Scarecrow Studies in Young Adult Literature
Series Editor: Patty Campbell

Scarecrow Studies in Young Adult Literature is intended to continue the body of critical writing established in Twayne's Young Adult Authors Series and to expand it beyond single-author studies to explorations of genres, multicultural writing, and controversial issues in YA reading. Many of the contributing authors of the series are among the leading scholars and critics of adolescent literature, and some are YA novelists themselves.

The series is shaped by its editor, Patty Campbell, who is a renowned authority in the field, with a thirty-year background as critic, lecturer, librarian, and teacher of young adult literature. Patty Campbell was the 2001 winner of the ALAN Award, given by the Assembly on Adolescent Literature of the National Council of Teachers of English for distinguished contribution to young adult literature. In 1989 she was the winner of the American Library Association's Grolier Award for distinguished service to young adults and reading.

1. *What's So Scary about R.L. Stine?* by Patrick Jones, 1998.
2. *Ann Rinaldi: Historian and Storyteller*, by Jeanne M. McGlinn, 2000.
3. *Norma Fox Mazer: A Writer's World*, by Arthea J.S. Reed, 2000.
4. *Exploding the Myths: The Truth about Teens and Reading*, by Marc Aronson, 2001.
5. *The Agony and the Eggplant: Daniel Pinkwater's Heroic Struggles in the Name of YA Literature*, by Walter Hogan, 2001.
6. *Caroline Cooney: Faith and Fiction*, by Pamela Sissi Carroll, 2001.
7. *Declarations of Independence: Empowered Girls in Young Adult Literature, 1990–2001*, by Joanne Brown and Nancy St. Clair, 2002.
8. *Lost Masterworks of Young Adult Literature*, by Connie S. Zitlow, 2002.
9. *Beyond the Pale: New Essays for a New Era*, by Marc Aronson, 2003.
10. *Orson Scott Card: Writer of the Terrible Choice*, by Edith S. Tyson, 2003.
11. *Jacqueline Woodson: "The Real Thing,"* by Lois Thomas Stover, 2003.
12. *Virginia Euwer Wolff: Capturing the Music of Young Voices*, by Suzanne Elizabeth Reid, 2003.

Virginia Euwer Wolff

Capturing the Music of Young Voices

Suzanne Elizabeth Reid

*Scarecrow Studies in Young Adult
Literature, No. 12*

The Scarecrow Press, Inc.
Lanham, Maryland, and Oxford
2003

SCARECROW PRESS, INC.

Published in the United States of America
by Scarecrow Press, Inc.
A wholly owned subsidiary of
The Rowman & Littlefield Publishing Group, Inc.
4501 Forbes Boulevard, Suite 200, Lanham, Maryland 20706
www.scarecrowpress.com

PO Box 317
Oxford
OX2 9RU, UK

British Library Cataloguing in Publication Information Available

Library of Congress Cataloging-in-Publication Data

Reid, Suzanne Elizabeth.
  Virginia Euwer Wolff : capturing the music of young voices / Suzanne Elizabeth
Reid.
      p. cm. — (Scarecrow studies in young adult literature ; no. 12)
  Includes bibliographical references and index.
  ISBN 0-8108-4858-9 (alk. paper)
  1. Wolff, Virginia Euwer—Criticism and interpretation. 2. Young adult fiction,
American—History and criticism. I. Title. II. Series. III. Series: Scarecrow
studies in young adult literature ; 12.
PS3573.O5613 Z86 2003
813'.54—dc21

                                                          2003010897

⊗™ The paper used in this publication meets the minimum requirements of
American National Standard for Information Sciences—Permanence of
Paper for Printed Library Materials, ANSI/NISO Z39.48-1992.
Manufactured in the United States of America.

In honor of Virginia Euwer Wolff and
Robin Lanier Reid for their
respectful use of language

~

Contents

Acknowledgments

As before, I am extremely grateful to Patty Campbell for offering me this opportunity to learn about an extraordinarily dedicated writer and her work. I also appreciate the helpful comments, questions, and corrections of Virginia Euwer Wolff, who graciously gave her time and attention to improving this work. Thank you to Debbie Whited for taking extra care in copying the photographs. Most of all and always, I thank my family for their constant loving support.

CHAPTER 1

~

Virginia Euwer Wolff: Teacher, Writer, and Artist

"I was held together by the violin. . . . It helped me from going over the brink of crying for days on end" (Bowlan, 5). Virginia Euwer Wolff refers to the sorrow she endured for years after her father died when she was five years old. Bereft of the linchpin of the family and emotionally scattered, haunted by a sense of chaotic uncertainty, she seems to have found a center through her practice of music and language. First in her youth, and again, in later life, she has clung to the hard discipline of trying again and again and again until her fingers find the right place on the strings and her bow arm the exact pressure and sweep, until the notes become recognizable music.

Learning to play the violin takes stubborn persistence; you slog through the squeaks and squalls, the not-quite-rightness of it all, but the reward lifts your spirit when you can intimate a sense of beautiful possibilities. There is a sense of celebration and joy when the grind of hard work approaches elegance. Virginia Euwer Wolff most often gets it right. Although she tends to speak of herself with modesty and self-dismissal, Wolff has obviously spent her lifetime refining the tones and precision of her language.

Music was not the only interest that held Virginia together. Her father had left behind his *Encyclopedia Britannica*, "gigantic green volumes." The young girl "chanted the gold titles on their bindings over and over again: "Mun to Pay, Pay to Ree, Ref to Shu, Shu to Tom. I must have been calling my father's name in the only way I knew how. I've spent the rest of my life trying to pull the secrets out of words" (Elleman, 1994), Wolff remembers.

The stories Wolff draws from her imagination seem as clear and as complicated as any retelling of recently lived experience. They seem as ordinary and as interesting as fresh gossip. Yet they also resonate with connections to age-old human experiences, to themes that pluck strings buried deeper than mere plots and events. She probes into the implications of death, fear, and disappointment. As painful and bleak as are some of the situations she describes in meticulous detail, her works ultimately gleam with hope. In the end, her characters find paths toward joy and connection. The compositions of Virginia Euwer Wolff are memorable for the uniqueness of their plots. She experiments with the traditional format of the novel as she seeks to braid rhythm and meaning.

Virginia's life story begins in Portland, Oregon, on August 25, 1937. "I was born into a loved and loving home," writes Wolff (1998, 300). After practicing law for several years in Pittsburgh, Pennsylvania, her father, Eugene Courtney Euwer, abandoned that world to move west. Without the benefit of the chainsaw, he cleared seventy acres of old-growth Douglas fir and cedar forest in order to plant an apple and pear orchard in sight of Mt. Hood, a peak always topped with snow. With a work crew, he built a massive, log house three miles from town, on the side of a mountain. A huge stone fireplace and generous windows gave the house light; heat came from a large cooking stove, and water from a tower behind the house. Unique in design and rather elegant, the house lacked electricity, but did include the luxuries of a grand piano, a library of books, and "views of more mountains than many people ever see in their lifetimes. It was a wonderful place for a childhood to happen in" (Gallo, 8).

An extensive collection of art on the walls included many pastels and watercolor landscapes from her uncle Anthony Euwer, who was renowned for his regional landscapes, as well as for his humorous verse. Virginia's mother was a fine pianist, so there were pleasures for the ear as well as for the eye and the mind. Daily life must have seemed full and good and secure. Unfortunately, Virginia barely remembers the voice of her father. Seventeen years older than her mother, he died of a heart attack in 1942 when Virginia was only five years old and her brother seven. "Suddenly the world that just the day before made sense to us went kerplooey, got incoherent" (Wolff 1998, 300).

"Ginny," as she was then called by her family, stopped eating and developed rickets. Perhaps she was desperate to gain at least some control over her world. Virginia remembers that suddenly her whole family "was in a tizzy" (Gallo, 9), rallying around her with hugs, visits to specialists in Portland, Oregon, and lots of other attentions. Her mother's parents lived in the nearby town where Virginia attended school and provided a second home where she could walk for lunch. Virginia also remembers listening to a lot of Brahms and other classical music on their wind-up Victrola record player.

Although the symptoms of rickets and her eating disorder seemed to disappear within a few years, and she never suffered any other major illness during her childhood, remnants of the shocking loss of her father have remained part of how Virginia experiences the world. "I am quite a different person from the person I would have been had my father lived through at least my childhood. . . . Every later loss seems to ride on top of that early one, and so those later experiences are different too" (Gallo, 9). How can a young woman feel secure about who she is or what she should do in her life if the authority in her life suddenly disappears? Much of Wolff's writing reflects a deeply set queasiness about the concept of happiness, that confident assumption that everything will work out just fine without much thought or effort. Her characters struggle against easy answers and against common notions about what is right and wrong. Like cultural heroes in the Western world since Odysseus, they enter an energetic struggle to find new answers and to discover their own moral paths.

Many of Wolff's characters also have to deal with the sudden loss of a close relative or friend, just as did Virginia. And, in similar fashion, her characters succeed in breaking through the numbing paralysis of grief by working hard at something that directs their attention outward, whether it is music or the study of amphibians or a dream of college. Finally, her characters learn about themselves by pushing out against their pain. Like Virginia, they eventually reach toward goals they might not have achieved except for their path through pain.

A great source of strength at this time was Virginia's mother, a former schoolteacher and Camp Fire Girls executive. Though diminutive in stature, Florence Craven Euwer obviously had a strong backbone. Even though the farm had no electricity, Virginia's mother learned how to run the orchard while, at the same time, serving on the school board, playing the organ at the Presbyterian church, and acting as "arbiter of good manners and good taste and kindness to people less fortunate than we." Virginia remembers, "She never split an infinitive that I ever found out about. The parlance in our home was of music and art and pets and harsh weather and love and Jesus" (Wolff 1998, 300–1). Wolff has another memory of her mother that demonstrates a gentler kind of courage: As a small child, soon after her father's death, she woke at night and discovered her mother in the kitchen, washing and bandaging the arm of a "dirty old reeking and bleeding fruit picker," drunk and injured in a knife fight; her mother was soothing him, "telling him he would be all right" (Wolff 1998, 307). Her mother was, above all, a busy woman, fully engaged in keeping their lives in order.

Soon after her father's death, her mother took Virginia and her brother to New York to visit relatives on an estate in Westchester County, near New York City. The family visited museums, Radio City Music Hall, and saw Rodgers and Hammerstein's musical *Oklahoma*. These expeditions were intellectually exciting and emotionally stimulating. When Virginia heard her cousin play the violin, she associated all the thrill and beauty of this New York City visit with his performance. She was struck by the glamorous shape and shine of the instrument, especially the play of light on its curves and gleaming wood. When her family returned home, Virginia begged to switch her piano lessons for instruction in playing the violin. Finally her mother relented, and her parents' strong love of music took hold of the young girl. Wolff's third book, *The Mozart Season*, is dedicated to both her mother and father.

Isolated in their mountain home three miles above the town where she would attend school, Virginia was immersed in classical music, literature, and the genteel language of her mother's family. "We were taught [to say] *umbilicus*, not *bellybutton*. *Buttocks*, not *hiny*" (Wolff 1998, 301). Although no kindergarten had been established, Virginia completed the other elementary grades in the town school. During her

Virginia at about age three in 1940 at her home in Valley Crest Orchards, Oregon. Her childhood was carefree until the death of her beloved father.

first year, she walked to her grandmother's house for lunch, and her first grade teacher treated her gently, as if to coax her out of her melancholy after her father's death. When Wolff was writing *Make Lemonade*, she gave her narrator two names: Verna LaVaughn. Verna, which has its roots in the Latin word for spring, was the first name of her first grade teacher, one of those who was so kind to her and never let her know that she was the last child in the class to learn to read (personal communication, 14 Oct. 2002, 3).

Her brother Eugene, two and a half years older than Virginia, was protective of his younger sister, as much as she would let him be. A disciplined and morally upright boy, he strove to excel in the outdoor skills of the Oregon mountain life as well as in school. He seemed to feel a high degree of responsibility for his sister; perhaps he was trying to replace their missing father. With a reputation as a good student at school and demonstrating the signs of becoming a model citizen in the community, he also displayed a normal modicum of mischievousness, but only that.

Apparently more of a floater than an achiever, Virginia preferred the slang she heard from her friends to the grammatically correct diction of her mother's world. She also seemed to lack scholarly ambitions. An excellent speller with a background of books and literate conversation, she got good grades, but she didn't focus on intellectual exploration. During this time she read more of MAD magazine than classical literature. In contrast to the staunch and serious nature of her mother, Virginia seemed to prefer the superficial. She reminisces, "My teachers used to get SO exasperated with me, because I giggled my way through adolescence" (Authorchats, 4). She "ate a kazillion French fries and drank three kazillion milkshakes" (Gallo, 10). However, she was not completely without responsibility. During the summertime, she was employed as a camp counselor, a job that gave her some of the happiest memories of that era.

Virginia Euwer Wolff describes her adolescence as a time of messy confusion. Underneath her superficial glibness was a gaping hole of insecurity. Why couldn't she be happy like everyone else seemed? Why did her father have to die? Who was she . . . and who would she become? As a teenager, she practiced smoking, drinking beer, and flirting. The Presbyterian services she had attended as a child now seemed boring and irrelevant, and her mother, whom she had adored and respected, now seemed impossibly dense about the purpose of life. What held her together during this time of relentless questioning was her music. Of her teenage years, she has said, "Music was gravity in my life" (Gallo, 10). Taking violin lessons and playing in youth orchestras kept her feet on the ground when everything else seemed to be swaying and uncertain.

Virginia's mother, somewhat older than most other parents and isolated by her highly educated tastes and thoughtful morality, most likely felt the same kind of frustration that most single parents with a strong sense of responsibility feel in rearing spirited teenagers. She chose to send Virginia to an Episcopal boarding school, in hopes that her daughter would become more self-disciplined and ladylike. At sixteen and at the beginning of her junior year, Virginia was not particularly interested in propriety; being a "lady" did not seem an attractive occupation or a worthy goal. Virginia became increasingly expert in those skills so abhorrent to her mother—smoking, drinking, and flirting. Although she was certainly not particularly wild by today's standards, nevertheless Virginia continued smoking, drinking, dating, and questioning established religion. Her first novel, *Rated PG*, was published in 1980 by St. Martin's Press, and may be described as a fictionalized autobiography, as the chronology seems to closely parallel Virginia's life at this time. She has called her time at this school "a constant pajama party" (Gallo, 12).

As emotionally difficult as this time might have been for Virginia, she was beginning to develop the habits of intellectual exploration that would lead to her writing such a variety of books later on. Virginia had always been a relatively slow reader, but her innate sense of correct spelling and syntax had pleased teachers enamored of grammar, and the knowledge she had gleaned from her house full of books endeared her to those teachers who valued literacy. She had always received good grades in English classes. Although she had read only a few classics, she had been deeply touched by several modern authors. Those whose influence would become lasting included J. D. Salinger, Ernest Hemingway, and F. Scott Fitzgerald. Salinger's *Catcher in the Rye* (1951) became a touchstone for many young readers of Virginia's generation. His book released them from the heavy wet blanket of traditional literary language. It captured the language of the post–World War II adolescent heart, partly a combination of judgmental irreverence toward middle-class conventional manners that seemed insincere and meaningless, and, juxtaposed against this scornful superiority, a deep yearning for the ignorant innocence and security of childhood. In her novel *Rated PG*, Wolff describes the main character's first encounter with Salinger's novel: "Into the thirsty stretches of my Presbyterian girlhood two portentous figures strayed, within a month of each other. One was a book and one was a person. . . . I was fifteen and in the advanced stages of illiteracy when I wandered into a rummage sale on a June afternoon in Oregon" (5). The book was Salinger's *Catcher in the Rye*. Captivated by the first sentence, she reads and rereads the book until her vision seems permanently changed. The town parades and the local citizens she had always admired seem sentimental and silly. She is disappointed that neither her best friend of many sympathetic years nor her universally admired older brother is equally impressed by Holden Caulfield's quest for innocence.

Bitsy, the central character in Wolff's novel, is soon afterward attracted to a college boy named Hayes who immediately recognizes her references to Salinger. Furthermore, his persona seems to reflect some of Caulfield's irreverent questioning and urbane intelligence. A month later, Bitsy discovers his copy of Salinger's *Nine Stories*, and reads "For Esmé—With Love and Squalor," about a serviceman stationed in England whose single conversation with a young thirteen-year-old girl named Esmé generates a letter from her that reaches him many weeks afterward. Although the war has officially ended, the young soldier's spirit appears to be intractably wounded. Esmé's package contains a watch, one of her few mementos from her father who had been slain in an early battle of the war. The profound generosity of this exceedingly intelligent young girl, so completely devoid of sentimentality or selfishness, is the beginning of the young soldier's healing. Salinger's characters are charmingly funny, intellectual, and unflappably brave; the story is deeply poignant for most readers, but for a young girl who had lost her own father and who had felt as emotionally dislocated as the soldier, the effect must have been almost painful. "More cruelty, more love than I could imagine exploded violently in my face," says the fictional Bitsy of *Rated PG*: "I'm completely changed. Clear down to my liver and everything" (40). The real-life Virginia Euwer Wolff has claimed that along with Gogol's "The Overcoat," J. D. Salinger's "For Esmé—With Love and Squalor" convinced her "in some utterly pre-verbal way" that writing was irrevocably important to her (Singer, 38).

At St. Helen's Hall, now known as the Oregon Episcopal School, Virginia reveled in the company of the more sophisticated friends she was meeting. Some had traveled, some had read widely, and many made a habit of questioning authority. The school's chaplain,

Father Evan Williams, became a mentor. He was "delighted to have a student who was reaching for ideas, however cockeyed" (Colburn, 55). Father Williams possessed the necessary intellectual courage to consider Virginia's challenges thoughtfully and then point her toward yet more paths to explore. It was Miss Irene Mate Campbell, Virginia's Latin teacher, who instilled in her an appreciation for "the endlessly intriguing connotative richness of words" (Gallo, 12). Years later, this sense of the semantic history of vocabulary is evident in Wolff's writing as, over and over again, she selects phrases and words that strike the reader as surprisingly precise; all the inferential tentacles of her language reach out to the right places in a reader's mind and heart.

Encouraged by her experiences at St. Helen's Hall to continue her intellectual adventures, Wolff began to read more widely and dig into intellectually deeper reading.

Virginia's uncle Anthony Euwer, an artist and limerick writer, made this bookplate showing Virginia's childhood home with a water tower behind it and Virginia and her brother with a dog in the front yard near a tree that was later the second largest dogwood in Oregon.

Salinger revealed to her the potential of language and the mysteries it could unveil. Reading Gogol gave her a sense of the rolling complexities possible in a grammatical sentence. Reading Arthur Miller showed her how a piece of literature could produce dramatic immediacy. She was accepted into the prestigious Smith College in western Massachusetts, three thousand miles away from her mountainside home in Oregon. With her habitual modesty, Wolff writes that she "got into Smith because of geographical distribution and because [she] played the violin" (Bowlan, 3). Her career at Smith stimulated a lifelong urge to learn, to study, and to strive to make a difference in the world. There she met people who thrilled her with their ideas and warmed her with their friendship.

One of these people was Jane Yolen, now a renowned writer for children and young adults, who lived in the same residence house during Wolff's sophomore year and impressed her with her vibrant energy and zest for expressing her interests and opinions. Wolff remembers her as a "very visible, dynamic young woman, much more interesting than most of us quiet 1950s girls were" (personal communication, 29 Oct. 2002). Many years later when Wolff began to try to write for publication, she sent Yolen a manuscript to read. Yolen, who has helped many new writers, introduced Wolff to her own literary agent, who has worked with her ever since. Wolff considers Yolen much more than a professional friend who knows the right people and the right paths for getting ahead in the literary world. Yolen's enthusiasm for learning and her generous sense of humor are a source of wisdom and comfort for Wolff in many aspects of her life.

While Virginia was at Smith, she played violin in the college orchestra, in some chamber ensembles, and accompanied some of the choirs in vesper services. Although Virginia had practiced and performed since she was about ten years old, she decided not to major in music or pursue it as a career. Always strictly clear about her own limitations, she has stated that "I knew by then I wasn't enough of a violinist to be a violinist" (Gallo, 13). Fortunately, she did not feel that way about her ambition to become a writer. Perhaps that is because, unlike many current authors, she had not spent much time writing beyond the usual classroom assignments during her youth. At Smith, she majored in English literature, studying many of the authors who would guide her thinking and her later work: Shakespeare, Anton Chekhov, Gerard Manley Hopkins, Kafka, Dylan Thomas, and, especially Nikolai Gogol. As a junior in college, her professor, George Gibian, introduced her to this author, his sentences that curl themselves into layered pockets of meaning, and his profoundly intimate portraits of characters dogged with the ironic awareness of how limited human vision can be in the face of life's vast possibilities. Wolff remembers that "it was Nikolai Gogol who set me back on my heels, excited and moved me, and whose influence I find ALL OVER my own work now" (personal communication, 12 March 2003).

Again, although it was not her major course of study, Virginia found that music acted as a steadying thread through the flux of new ideas and experiences. Her four years at Smith were not all rosy; like many college students, she had a sense of being different from the others. Nobody at St. Helen's Hall had remarked on the strangeness of her pronunciation. Nobody had made her feel that she lived beyond the fringe of cultural civilization. At Smith, she worked hard and learned much. Of those years, Virginia has said, "My Smith education . . . taught me essentially what Maya Angelou says: 'Preparation is rarely easy, and never beautiful'" (Bowlan, 3).

Soon after she graduated from college in 1959, Virginia Euwer married Art Wolff and the two moved to New York City to be close to the theater world of her husband. There she taught English in a junior high school in the Bronx for a year before taking time out to become the mother of their two children, Anthony Richard and Juliet Dianne. During that time, Wolff expressed her earnest belief in universal rights for all individuals through her active involvement in Another Mother for Peace. In 1968 she returned to teaching at a private school, the Miquon School in Philadelphia. Established in 1932, the school was based on the educational philosophy of John Dewey. Students were encouraged to learn the concepts of math, language, and science by participating in hands-on projects that were designed to be as much like out-of-school experiences as is possible in a classroom.

When the Wolffs moved back to New York City in 1972, Virginia taught small children in the Fiedel School on Long Island. Thus grew a career of widely varied teaching experiences that exposed her to a large range of students and classrooms, information that was helpful in her later writing about teaching and learning. In her 2002 speech to a conference of English teachers, she summed up her own career of more than thirty years in the classroom: "six years of little kids, ages five-eight; about three years of middle school kids; and twenty something years of high school English. . . . I've been to more faculty meetings than picnics in my life, have read more student essays than novels, . . . [and] written more lesson plans than book chapters" ("What we lose, what we find," 23 Nov. 2002).

The value of her experiences is particularly clear when she portrays the daily life of students. She gets the melody of school right, locating those notes that most students hear above and beyond the drone of many teachers. The dominant theme for most students is measured by where their peers place them on a social scale that seems to change key every day. Although Wolff's early writing did not particularly focus on her school experiences, she was obviously listening well.

The Wolff family moved twelve times in seventeen years to follow Art's career in theater and television. They lived in Connecticut, New York, Ohio, Pennsylvania, and Washington, D.C. In 1976, Virginia's marriage to Art ended in divorce. Of her relationship with her husband and the theater milieu in which they lived, she writes, "That era in my life gave me two terrific children, a permanent appetite for really great theater, and several people's lifetime supplies of four words: *incredible*, *fabulous*, *magnificent*, and *darling*" (Wolff 1998, 305).

At the same time, Virginia was also continuing her quest to achieve excellence as a professional writer. In 1974, she continued her education in creative writing at Long Island University where, in 1976, she won a prize in poetry. After a summer of further study at Warren Wilson College in the mountains of North Carolina, she moved to her home state, Oregon, where she took a job teaching English in a public high school in Hood River. The summer after, in 1977, she was lecturing on techniques of fiction writing at the Willamette Writers Conference.

Her identity as a "writer" was solidifying. By 1980 she had won two more awards, one for poems from the Oregon Teachers as Writers and one from *Williamette Week* for her story "Pole Beans for Rent." Several magazines, including *Ladies Home Journal* and *Seventeen*, published her stories and poetry. And St. Martin's Press had published her first novel, *Rated PG*, summarized above.

Although *Rated PG* was reviewed as sensitively written in a "lively and engaging style . . . characterized by surprising and appropriate metaphor" (Karen Pate, *Oregon* magazine, 1981), Wolff doesn't consider this part of her main oeuvre, especially now that she calls herself a "kids' author." "Thank goodness it went out of print" (Bowlan, 6). However, an element of her writing that has continued to attract critical notice is her ability to pull an unusual metaphor out of her writing hat. Her stylistic inventiveness and the precision with which she uses words amaze critical readers and charm the rest. And *Rated PG* does capture that enveloping joy of a sensitive adolescent's first love not only for another person, but also for the beauty of words and the excitement of good music. For me, reading it brought back memories of those thrilling moments when the world seems too full of joy to contain inside a single mind, juxtaposed, often within hours, with a smothering blanket of despair that presses out every inch of light. *Rated PG* certainly does not measure up to the literary inventiveness of Wolff's later books, but it has its own virtues. One of its most stunning metaphors reflects Wolff's musical interests: As the main character, teenaged Bitsy is swimming across the Columbia River on a summer afternoon: "the Sibelius Violin Concerto came zooming right down out of the sky, the second *largamente*, the one after the cadenza where it goes sweeping into double-stops in five flats, the way Heifetz played it, as if his violin would split wide open with passion and sweet grandeur" (26).

By 1980, Wolff was firm in her resolve to make writing a full-time career. At about this time, while she was registered in yet another writing class, author Mark Harris offered her advice that proved pivotal in her road toward professional success: "Stop filling up your time taking classes. Your job is to sit in your chair and write" (Gallo, 26). Wolff has described her younger self as feeling inept and scared: "I was a scared kid. I was a scared young adult. I was a terrified wife and an apprehensive mother" (Bowlan, 9). But this tentativeness gave her the time to learn life deeply while she gleaned the courage to express her ideas in writing.

By the time she wrote her first young adult novel, *Probably Still Nick Swansen* (Henry Holt), in 1988, she had lived through almost fifty years of wondering "What am I supposed to do with my life?" and "How?"

and "Why?" Wolff believes that suffering through difficult situations and asking these hard questions is the way to learn those lasting lessons in life that resonate with a wide range of readers.

Because she thinks through these questions slowly, perhaps more thoroughly than most people, she has often felt out of step in a world that expects quick, facile answers. While she was acting as a mother and a schoolteacher, the constant demand for responsible attention "flustered the socks off [her]"; she reports that she was "always behind, always afraid I would be found out for not having done eight of the forty-eight things I was supposed to do" (Bowlan, 5).

That sense of working in a different rhythm from most people translated powerfully into the character of Nick Swansen, a young adolescent who has been diagnosed as learning-disabled. He struggles painfully with the social difficulties of living with a label in high school. By the end of the book, all of Nick's problems are not solved, but he has learned quite a bit about himself and how he can cope with the less than ideal social world of his milieu.

This book challenged Wolff's idea of herself as an inept writer when it received many awards, including the *School Library Journal*'s "Best Book" award in 1988. It was also the recipient of the International Reading Association Young Adult Book Award, and a Booklist Editor's Choice in the same year. Subsequently, it was also listed as one of the 100 Best of the Best Books for Young Adults published between 1967 and 1992, and a YALSA Popular Paperback for Young Adults in 1999. However, these honors certainly did not swell her head as they might have other writers. Nor did they tempt her to relax her efforts. "I'm a farm girl," Wolff explains. "I can't bask" (Colburn, 54). Rather, she is severely self-critical: "When I was writing *Probably Still Nick Swansen*, I didn't know that it was a particular *kind* of young adult book: the standard story of a lonely Outsider who has the grit to survive. . . . Like so many beginning writers, I made the erroneous assumption that no one had ever done what I was doing" (Wolff 1998, 305). While it is true that traditional themes have been "done" before, many times, there can never be too many excellent books that are easy to read but well-written, imaginatively conceived, and deeply felt. Traditional themes in books such as these touch readers' hearts and speak to their minds afresh. The message of surviving social pain by persisting day by day needs to be heard by many people quite often. Resilience is a skill that takes practice, and vicarious examples fortify readers (not just the young!) who see themselves in the pages of a powerfully written story and drink in necessary lessons that build hope.

Wolff had intended to quit teaching in public high school to follow the advice of writing instructor Mark Harris and write full-time. However, an unusual opportunity extended her teaching career. Mt. Hood Academy, on the slopes of one of the tallest mountains in North America, offered her a unique part-time position that included a season ski pass. The academy is a place for young high-school-age athletes with a passion for skiing so strong that many are training for the Olympics. In November, they come from their high schools to the academy and train until March, taking an individualized curriculum of academic subjects along with their skiing classes. Although the task of teaching a number of students, each with separate needs, is incredibly challenging, Wolff thrived on the opportunity to encourage these competitive athletes to express their ideas and observations with flair and verve. Wolff is particularly proud of their creative writing journals. From these students, Wolff learned that the way to succeed at either skiing or writing is to persist: "When you have a disappointing run, you pick yourself up and you do it again to see if you can do it better. And again. And again" (Gallo, 14).

Her next book, *The Mozart Season*, focuses on a young girl whose life is not that different from these athletes who devote so much of their time and energy to developing and perfecting a skill. Allegra seems to have all that Nick Swansen feels he lacks—good friends with similar interests, confident parents who know how to help her achieve her goals, and a life filled with the music she loves. She is surrounded by people who admire not only her extraordinary ability to play the violin, but also her tendency to empathize with people in trouble. Allegra too must struggle to understand what is expected of her, and she too experiences frustration and disappointment when learning doesn't come easily. Published by Holt in 1991 and reissued by Scholastic in 1993, this book was named an American Library Association (ALA) Notable Book for Children and an ALA Best Book for Young Adults.

In *The Mozart Season*, Wolff draws on her experiences as a violinist and a lover of classical music. The choice of violin as an instrument was

ironic for a person such as Wolff, who tends not to tolerate less than excellent performance in any of her endeavors, as it is one of the most difficult and demanding musical instruments to learn. However, it is part
of Wolff's persistent nature to push against intimidating circumstances
not just to the point of succeeding but until she gets it right according
to her own high standards.

It is this special element of persistence that Wolff explored in *Make
Lemonade* (Holt, Scholastic, 1993), the story of a fourteen-year-old girl
living in an impoverished inner-city neighborhood that threatens to
blight any chance for success because of its easy access to drugs, early
pregnancy, violence, and despair. Verna LaVaughn and her mother
hope for more. At the beginning of the book, LaVaughn is seeking a
part-time job to build a college fund. The job she finds is to babysit for
two-year-old Jeremy and his baby sister Jilly while their mother, Jolly,
goes off to work. LaVaughn finds that her own circumstances seem easy
compared to the filth and uncertainty in Jolly's life. Using the common
sense of her mother and information from her Life Skills class in school,
LaVaughn strives to help Jolly "take hold" of life. At the same time,
LaVaughn struggles to keep a balance between helping her new friend
and working toward her own dreams.

It took a great deal of courage to write such an unconventional book
as *Make Lemonade*. Narrated by LaVaughn, it is written in a format that
looks like poetry, with lines that break according to where her thoughts
hesitate, rather than according to preset margins. She tells her story in
language that sounds, to many critics, like inner-city slang, but Wolff
doesn't reveal her character's ethnicity or even her last name. The city
could be anywhere in the United States, and, given the widespread proliferation of language patterns through popular media, LaVaughn's
speech patterns are not necessarily identifiable as particularly inner
city. At least one reader, one of my students in rural Appalachia,
thought that LaVaughn sounded like "just a country girl."

While Wolff was writing the book, she began to realize how unconventional it was, and how much criticism she might receive from reviewers. For an author relatively new to publishing, she was taking a
tremendous risk. What had finally given Wolff the courage to write
such a book? While she was writing *The Mozart Season*, she attended a
clinic to learn how to stop smoking. This made such a difference in her

confidence that her instructor appears in the acknowledgements of that book. She believed that if she could beat her addiction to cigarettes, she might also be able to overcome her desperate fear of speaking in public. And if she could do that, she could write using her own unique style.

A further motivation is her lifelong dedication to finding and expressing young voices who might not otherwise be heard. Virginia has been closely involved with young people all her life, during her teaching career, in the musical ensembles and orchestras with whom she practices and performs, and, now, through her appearances as an author. She has great empathy for these young people, and recognizes their needs. "There are girls out there who need this book, I hope, and I'm writing it for them. I'm not writing it for reviewers" (Bowlan, 7). In the end, Wolff kept loyal to the voice of LaVaughn who came to her seemingly from nowhere. *Make Lemonade* is tremendously successful; it won *Booklist's* Top of the List Award in 1993. Since then, this innovative work has been admired by both educational professionals and young readers as a book with great impact.

In her list of acknowledgements in *Make Lemonade,* Wolff gives thanks "most emphatically to Brenda Bowen," her editor, for supporting the risks she takes in her writing. In her next book, *Bat 6,* she gives thanks to Ms. Bowen "feather by feather." This is a reference to Anne Lamott's book on writing, *Bird by Bird.* However, a secondary reference could be Emily Dickinson's poem "Hope is a thing with feathers." Wolff has written a preface to a collection of Dickinson's poetry, and this would be a most appropriate allusion to the book *Bat 6,* a work with a most unusual genesis.

After the publication of *Make Lemonade,* Wolff was increasingly well regarded as a writer of young adult literature and was often invited to attend conferences and to address general audiences about literature. At one conference she met Don Gallo, who has generated a renewed interest in young adult short stories by compiling more than seven volumes. He sent Wolff a postcard, challenging her to write a short story about a subject she had never approached, a story for his collection *Ultimate Sports: Short Stories by Outstanding Writers for Young Adults* (1995). As Wolff began her assignment, she was struck with a vision of a crowd of people running toward first base. As she wrote, she realized that she was writing what eventually became the novel *Bat 6*, an experimental montage of voices that merge into the story, leading up to a cruel act motivated by racist hatred.

Several adult critics had referred to implied racism in *Make Lemonade*, a reference that irked Wolff, who had consciously avoided any explicit reference to ethnic identity. Part of her motivation for expanding the impetus for *Bat 6* into a book was her impatience with glib and superficial references to race. Why did adult readers assume that any character that lived in inner-city poverty was black? "These are raceless kids who I hope are universal enough that they don't have a defining set of racial characteristics. You want race? I'll give you race" (Bowlan, 10).

The racist act that inspired *Bat 6* grew out of the tremendous suspicion of all Asians during World War II, particularly in the Northwest and California. This fear of invasion by Japanese troops, and a tendency to stereotype anyone who seemed foreign to mainstream culture, led ultimately to the internment of many Asians by the U.S. government. In Wolff's book, the softball players are young adolescent girls who reflect their parents' ethics and the stories they hear in the years immediately following World War II as they prepare to compete in an annual softball game between schools in small-town Oregon. The small community seems safe and friendly until a sudden act of violence against a young player of Japanese descent shocks the girls and their parents into realizing the destructive depth of racial thinking.

The book is not easy to read, partly because of the number of voices represented in the script as each girl tells her version of the story. It is also not easy to face up to Wolff's unrelenting insistence that we recognize our own culpability when anyone of our community is hurt. *Bat 6* won't let the reader avoid the realization that racism has tentacles that reach into unexpected corners of innocent minds. That is discouraging news for readers who want to pretend that racism is simple. Despite the powerful impact of *Bat 6*, it did not receive as many awards as her other books, but Wolff was especially gratified by its winning the Jane Addams award, given to books that strive to promote peace and equality.

The short story that Wolff did write for Don Gallo's *Ultimate Sports* as sort of a "Plan B" (Gallo, 18) is "Brownian Motion," about scuba diving, one of several athletic skills with which Wolff can claim acquaintance. Another of Wolff's short stories also deals with the lasting destructiveness of racism. "The Un-numbing of Cory Willhouse" was included in *No Easy Answers: Short Stories About Teenagers Making Tough Choices* (1997), which was also edited by Gallo. Fifteen-year-old Cory is riddled by guilt, particularly for stealing from a Korean market on Halloween night when he was nine years old and was part of a foursome bent on making trouble. Six years later when he hears that the store has been burned down, Cory feels that he can rid himself of his remaining uncomfortable shreds of remorse by helping the Korean owner rebuild. He spends hours working with the family, even cutting back on his sports. Although the family's gratitude scratches at his guilt, he is still more discomforted at their coldness after he admits that he had once been one of their young tormentors. The story of Cory is a perceptive description of the long shadow that one shameful act can throw. To capture this horrible inner malaise Wolff reached back to her fifth grade days for a memory of being a not-so-innocent bystander of a deed she knew to be wrong, and translated it to a current context.

Wolff has strong ideas about literature. Reading works of literature by writers who have mastered their craft, she believes, builds "an accumulating sense of language" (Bowlan, 6) that helps her avoid shallow perceptions and tired metaphors and images. For her, sloppy writing is a waste of a reader's time. Wolff writes slowly because she struggles continually, first to find the right scope for her ideas, and then to elaborate them so they work on more than one level.

Her writing does not usually derive from a plotline or any particular plan. She tends to dive into writing around a vision that has come to her like a dream, or voices she hears in her head, or a memory. *Bat 6* began with a vision of a crisis at the end of a softball game: players, officials, and onlookers streaming toward first base—something obviously wrong (Sutton, 286). *The Mozart Season* was inspired by watching a string quartet playing outside, each player with a page-turner. The image of a young person standing outside the windows of a dance, all dressed up with no-place to go, was the impetus for *Probably Still Nick Swansen*.

Once she decides to develop one of her visions or ideas, she selects the appropriate format. Will her story become a short story, or will it stretch into a novel? When she teaches writing, she tells her students that a short story is "usually not a profound character study. And it is usually not a one-liner stretched thin like bubble gum. . . . [T]he richness of a short story is what may come back to us in car-stopping flashes, weeks or years later, whereas the richness of a novel is the kind that never truly leaves us" (Singer, 38). If Wolff feels that her idea deserves the years of hard labor and intensive attention that will be necessary for the kinds of books she writes, she goes on to the next step, which is to find the voice (or voices) of the story. Characters should speak in rhythms and combinations that reflect their innermost psychology and motivations. It is because of Wolff's deep awareness of sounds and her experience with the art of sound, music, that the voices of her books vary so widely.

With characteristic humility, Wolff explains why she listens to classical music while she composes her fiction. "If I don't have music, I'm half a brain. Because I don't think I have much to say, but when I'm combining some little impulses in my mind with the great ideas I'm hearing across the room from the great minds of the past, then I find that I *do* have something to say" (Sutton, 285). Music is her inspiration, the medium she uses to garner new thoughts. Either the pieces she hears invoke memories from a lifetime of listening closely to music, or they color her intellect with their sensual and emotional qualities, or perhaps both. Perhaps the melodic lines and rhythmic impulses of classical music are connected with the creation of poetic language in more ways than have been traditionally defined.

Playing music teaches Wolff how to craft a work of art from the raw material of sounds and image. Her stories may begin with an improvisation or an idea that seems spontaneous, but she spends as much effort and time refining and shaping it into a plot with texture as she might spend practicing new music. Recurring motifs add texture to her writing and satisfy a reader's need for pattern. Wolff credits her experience playing chamber music with the strengthening of her awareness that each participant in a story has a distinctive voice that needs to be heard. Her participation in various musical ensembles has given her a sense of when each voice needs to enter into the conversation, a sense of the balance and timing of all the voices. Learning new music and new interpretations reminds her of the necessity for constructive criticism, as harsh or intrusive as it might seem at times.

Knowing about the struggles of her favorite music composers helps her keep writing problems in perspective. When she encounters a block in her writing, she reminds herself of Beethoven's deafness or Mahler's grief for his dying daughter. Wolff also believes that the emotional impact of classical music is related to our inherent consciousness of its "overwhelming sense of tragedy. . . . Even the lightest of music always has that underside that we're going to die" (Sutton, 285).

Perhaps because of the early shock of her father's death, Wolff seems to enjoy a melancholic bent; she appreciates the minor keys of life. As early as her writing of *Rated PG*, she described her main character as someone who "luxuriates in the symphony of my own tears and the noise of the river" (40). Her introduction to *"I'm nobody! Who are you?" Poems by Emily Dickinson* (Mesmer, 2002) explains that exploring life by "surrounding" it with language is the purpose of poetry. Often exploring or examining one's life, as Socrates recommended, can lead to embarrassment and melancholy, but these feelings are certainly not fatal. Wolff believes that the harder experiences in life are probably the most enlightening. In her writing, she avoids simplistic happy solutions: "I'm trying to teach that we learn only through pain, which is what I finally figured out in my life. The things that have been happy and triumphant have not taught me very much. The things that were difficult and defeating—those are the things I've learned from" (Bowlan, 4). Wolff is not so much a pessimist as a believer in self-sufficiency who is cautiously hopeful about life. She is grateful for each day of life when she can work in her studio with its framed quotations, sitting in a chair from her grandmother's music room and watching birds float by. She is grateful when nobody has been hurt or has died at the end of the day, and when she can record in her calendar that she has achieved a bit more writing.

If Wolff is not a cheerful optimist who expects a life without pain, her belief in human resilience is strong. She believes that individual achievement is mostly a habit of daily dogged persistence; "Of course you're going to get knocked down. Life is that way. What are you going to do to pick yourself up?" (Bowlan, 5).

Wolff uses music, hard work, continuing study of classical literature, and a collection of commemorative coffee mugs to urge her on toward her goals. She keeps notebooks on each book, recording her progress, her questions, and also little notes of self-congratulation. These notes sometimes grow to volumes longer than the book; they serve as running commentary on her work.

In 1998 Wolff retired from classroom teaching and now writes full-time. Physically active as well as mentally adventurous, she has taught swimming and worked as a lifeguard. When she isn't writing, she likes to hike, swim, and ski cross-country. She enjoyed downhill skiing until she had an accident on the slopes that now keeps her on more level ground.

Her renown as an author brings frequent requests for interviews, letters, and guest lectures at schools and literature conferences. Her years of teaching have made her conscientious about her responses to students of all ages; she expends a great deal of care and effort in crafting the lessons she teaches through these venues. What are these lessons? Life may be full of sadness and loneliness, but it can also be filled with joy. Joy comes from practicing compassion toward others. It comes from the hard and persistent mastery of an art, a skill, or a body of knowledge. It comes from living deeply, honestly, and honorably.

Outside of the cottage where she lives, set near a creek bordered by ferns and forest, she likes to garden when she is not traveling. Wolff continues practicing her music, performing as a violinist with the Oregon Sinfonetta, an orchestra; Parnassius, a piano quintet; and occasionally as

Wolff's study in her home in Oregon City where she creates her books, surrounded by inspiring mementos.

a substitute in other groups. She writes that she cannot imagine a better life for herself, one that is made up mostly of writing and music. Her son Tony, a professional jazz guitarist, and her daughter Juliet, a psychotherapist, visit frequently. Wolff is pleased that her two grandchildren, Max and Sarah, are learning to enjoy the books she loved as a child.

Virginia Euwer Wolff has certainly earned a reputation as one of the leading authors of thought-provoking fiction for young adults. In an issue of *From the Middle* devoted to classifying recent young adult literature (as well as giving tributes to the teaching heroes of September 11), two of Wolff's books are annotated in articles reviewing different genres of good young adult literature. *Bat 6* is recommended as one of the "new releases that tackle unusual historical topics" (Pavonetti, 78), and *The Mozart Season* is recommended for gifted readers (Olenchak, 72). Had the journal been printed one month later, two of her other books would most likely have been mentioned: *Make Lemonade* as an example of a novel in verse format (despite Wolff's valid claims to the contrary), "the newest—and arguably most exciting trend in the ongoing poetry renaissance" (Cart, 97), and *True Believer* as the winner of the National Book Award in 2001.

References

AuthorChats, 5 Dec. 2001.

Bowlan, Cheryl. "Interview with Eugene Euwer Wolff," in *Contemporary Authors Online*. (The Gale Group, 2001). http://www.galenet.com (3 Jan. 2002), 3.

Cart, Michael. "From Insider to Outsider: The Evolution of Young Adult Literature," *Voices from the Middle* 9, no. 2 (December 2001).

Colburn, Nell. "The Incomparable Wolff," *School Library Journal* 48, no. 2 (February 2002).

Elleman, Barbara. *Books Change Lives*. American Library Association, 1994.

Gallo, Don. "Virginia Euwer Wolff." Authors4Teens.com, http://www.authors4teens.com/A4T?source=interview&authorid=wolff (16 Jan. 2001).

Olenchak, Richard F. "When Gifted Readers Hunt for Books," *Voices from the Middle* 9, no. 2 (December 2001).

Pavonetti, Linda M. "Historical Fiction—New and Old," *Voices from the Middle* 9, no. 2 (December 2001).

Singer, Marilyn. "What is a Short Story?" *The ALAN Review* 28, no. 1 (Fall 2000).

Sutton, Roger. "An Interview with Virginia Euwer Wolff," The Horn Book 77, no. 3 (May/June 2001).

Transcript from 2001 Book Awards. National Book Foundation, http://209. 67.253.214/nbf/docs/nba01_speech_wolff.htm (10 Jul. 2002).

Wolff, Virginia Euwer. "If I Was Doing It Proper, What Was You Laughing At?" The Horn Book 74, no. 3 (May 1998).

Wolff, Virginia Euwer. Rated PG. New York: St. Martin's Press, 1980.

Wolff, Virginia. "What We Lose, What We Find" speech, ALAN-NCTE, Atlanta, Ga., 23 Nov. 2002.

CHAPTER 2

∼

Probably Still Nick Swansen:
Living with a Different Mind

"When I began writing *Probably Still Nick Swansen,* I saw in my mind a boy standing outside a building with all kinds of happiness, bright lights, and music going on within, and what was playing outside for him, his own private song, was 'Eleanor Rigby' " (Sutton, 285), explains Wolff. "I just had a story. . . . I really didn't know if what I was writing would turn out to be a novel or a short story [or] . . . a poem" (Zvirin, 1250). The story turned out to be a novel about the boy standing outside the window and how he adapts to his disappointment. This boy also has to adjust to the reality that the people around him consider him abnormal, not quite capable of fitting into the regular classes in school and of making his own decisions. Is Nick actually capable of selecting and remembering relevant information and then making appropriate decisions? Will he never mature into an adult who can live independently of his parents or other caretakers? Will he always need "special" help?

The main character of this book, Nick Swansen, is hampered by "minimal brain dysfunction," a term that may be dated but that accurately describes his general slowness in processing new information. But Wolff's novel is not a treatise about students with medical disabilities. It is more a fictional dive into the dramatic world of high school. Wolff's research focused more on learning how to use the voice of a boy than on obstacles to learning. In an interview she explains how her ideas came partly from overhearing a conversation about a student who had eagerly anticipated an event, and then, a few days later, had been disappointed. "I major in disappointment," declares Wolff. "I guess Nick Swansen was basically me" (Zvirin, 1251)·. If Wolff is, in part, portraying her own insecurities about how to communicate accurately, she is displaying amazing courage in revealing a side that most of us keep buried deep beneath words. In the character of Nick, she exposes the kind of language we use when we are unsure of our perceptions. People who are skeptical about the predictability of their world tend to hesitate before making a judgment or committing an opinion to any but the most general statements. They tend to leave room for escape in their conclusions, and add all sorts of qualifications to their pronouncements. Because contemporary American culture values decisiveness and quick responses, this tentativeness of speech can be interpreted as a lack of intelligence. However, for many people this hesitancy is merely lack of confidence in the steadfastness of reality as we think we know it.

In an interview, Wolff has described Nick as "a valid person, in fact quite an appealing person. He simply doesn't speak the coded language of the In-group. He's a nice kid who just doesn't get it as fast as others do" (Wolff, 299). Wolff was never an official special education teacher, nor is her son learning-disabled, as some readers have imagined. Her empathy for Nick may partly come from her own insecurities about learning and using language precisely and correctly. As a self-described "slow thinker" who, in past years, felt flustered by the many constant demands of motherhood and teaching, Wolff is perhaps using Nick's tentative language to reflect her own frustrations at feeling rushed when she is trying to create language that measures up to her high standards of exact meaning and truthful sound. This book is her attempt to help us live within the mind of a person who is physically normal yet whose ability to easily express his ideas and emotions is muffled or awkwardly thwarted by his insecurities.

"Be yourself" is both the best advice and the most useless advice a young adult can hear. Who is "yourself"? How can you "be" something you don't understand? Most young children are themselves, noticing and responding to their environment without much judgment or categorization. In the beginning of *Probably Still Nick Swansen*, Wolff portrays the hero's mind as childlike; Nick admits to having little consciousness that he himself can direct his fate, much less the lives of people around him. We see his world through simple declarative sentences with little description or elaboration. Like a child, he personifies inanimate objects: "Room 19 was dressed up. It crackled with sounds and party smells came from everywhere" and "A giant homemade poster was trying to come unhinged" (1). Objects and people seem to share the same motivations and importance to Nick.

The party is a farewell event for Shana, who is leaving the Special Ed class to participate in regular classes, "Going Up," as Nick calls it. We get a sense of Nick's limited math skills when he figures out that he has been in Special Ed for three years, from age fourteen, then fifteen, and now sixteen.

Nick's sentences are not only grammatically simple; his logic is more sequential than abstract. He likes Shana because "she was nice when she smiled, and she smiled a lot" (4). Although he has just realized that his father's reference to a "garlic-bread zone" was a joke, he still believes that his older sister Dianne "never found that out" (7).

In describing Nick's befuddlement, Wolff harkens back to her own childhood experience with Winnie the Pooh books. When Nick's mother reads to him about Eeyore's broken birthday presents, he does not understand the irony: The habitually gloomy donkey Eeyore actually enjoys the broken toys more than he might have in their original form. Wolff admits that, like Nick, "I never got the joke about Eeyore until I was much older; I thought he really was unlucky, and all those terrible things were really happening to him." She was much older before she finally understood that the world would judge Eeyore as "just a self-pitying fool" (Zvirin, 1251). Nick too, sympathizes with Eeyore, weeping over the donkey's supposed disappointment at the inappropriate gift. Neither child had the ironic detachment and the experienced worldview that would let them congratulate Eeyore for making the best of what he had, whether or not his gifts were valued by the world in general. Nick did sense that he might be "terribly weird to worry so much about that party" (5). What is a bit weird is his almost obsessive need to justify his thoughts to himself and, thus, the reader; his lack of trust in his own perceptions is extreme.

Although Nick seems not to think critically about what he sees, we know that he can make good decisions about his behavior; when a classmate pokes him by mistake, he doesn't retaliate. He is sensitive, crying about Eeyore's supposedly hurt feelings and worrying that the balloon he hands to Shana might break and ruin the fun. He is gentle, perhaps even passive: When another classmate grabs the balloon from him, he just lets it go. And when Shana flirts with him by calling him mature, he mentally protests: "He wasn't mature. He wasn't anything, just somebody alive, that was all" (13). At this point Nick is reluctant to assume the responsibility of defining himself independently, of deciding how he fits into the scheme of life as he knows it. At the core of his being, he feels incapable of making good decisions.

At this point in our introduction to Nick, Wolff's writing has become more complex, both grammatically and semantically. Now that we recognize that Nick's slowness of mind, what we usually call a "learning disability," keeps him from acting as an independent self, we are about to follow his progress toward maturity. Wolff's language mirrors that progress. The first signal that Nick isn't as "disabled" as he first has seemed is the question he writes on Shana's balloon, "Where is up?" Nick claims that the words just happened to be floating through his mind when it was his turn to write on the balloon, but Shana recognizes the thought as somewhat profound, abstract, and mature. Laughing in appreciation, she predicts that his turn to rise out of Special Ed will come soon; "Just keep morking" (14), she advises, reminding him of a time when they both recognized the spelling error of another student whose propensity for shoplifting has cut his classroom career short.

Is Nick's cognitive ability impaired? Is his passive nature innate and does it cause the slowness of his learning? Or is his hesitancy a sign of the shock to his mental development when he witnessed the death of his sister when he was only five years old? Like the author, Nick, at a very young age, had suffered the loss of a family member; his sister drowned in a pool while he was watching. His whole image of how the world works must have crumpled in the space of those ten minutes. His sister had been older than he was, smarter than he has ever felt, his guide and mentor in how to react to other people. He idolized her, depended on her, and trusted her to ask the questions he could not artic-

ulate, to express the feelings he could not describe, and to show him
how to act among his peers and the adults in their world.

Now, years later, Nick still thinks about his sister Dianne, wondering what she would look like, and trying to imagine how she
would answer his questions about how to survive in high school. But
he has conflicting emotions about remembering her. On the one
hand, "talking" with her in his mind helps him sort out his perceptions. He needs to know about his feelings for Shana, who has made
it obvious to him that she likes him more than the other boys. On
the other hand, remembering his sister stirs up the pain of her death.

Now that he is sixteen, however, Nick is beginning to think independently, though it makes him nervous to be acting on his own. He decides to ask Shana to the prom. Just as his teacher Mr. Norton has often
advised, he makes a list of all that he would have to do and all the questions he would have to answer. On the twentieth day before the prom,
he finally asks Shana and is surprised that she immediately answers
affirmatively, although she doesn't seem very enthusiastic at the time.

Suddenly, now that Nick has plans to accomplish, the other people
in Special Ed seem unimportant and uninteresting. The days rush by as
he practices dancing and works at the garden center to earn money to
pay for tickets, the corsage, and the boat ride. He finds that buying tickets makes him seem normal, just like the other kids in school. Then,
just as he is beginning to feel some confidence, his self-assurance is un-
dermined by a note that falls from Shana's book bag. "YOUR NOT IN
HIS CLASS ANYMORE ANYWAY" (26). However, he convinces
himself that Shana's smile means that "probably" there is "no problem"
(26), and the careless spelling makes the message seem careless or, at
least, ill-advised. Nick's nervousness grows as his teacher, Mr. Norton,
tries to give him advice about dating. Nick thinks, "If he wasn't Special
Ed., he'd know what to do and he'd know how to do it" (28). He even
suspects that God might be mocking his attempts to imagine Dianne's
answers to his questions.

Nick begins to panic as he pictures his sister returning from death
and not being able to recognize him as her little brother. Just as his
fright rises out of control, it is time for science, where he will work on
his beloved amphibian project. Wolff has mentioned that she believes
young people need an abiding interest in something in order to survive

psychologically the vicissitudes of living in these insecure times. Her own safety valve was her involvement with music; for Nick, it is a fascination with amphibians, and an ability to remember their scientific names and attributes, even though he has needed help with reading and spelling them. His favorite is the Pig frog, which he considers too pretty for the label it has been given. As Nick works with the slides of salamanders, memorizing new information, he feels more comfortable about the prom and about himself, remembering teachers' reassurances about how everyone has differences and difficulties with learning.

Excitement mounts on the day before the prom as Nick performs all the errands related to prom going. Wolff's sly humor bubbles out as Nick describes his visit with Shana's mother. After he has taken such care to protect the corsage from damage during his bike ride, once he hands it over to Shana's mother, he has to watch her wave it around like a precariously balanced marionette as she tries to negotiate photographers around a half-finished house and seems only vaguely to remember that her daughter has a date with Nick. Nick decides she is hyperactive, and he tries to practice the tolerance for differences in behavior that he has been taught in Special Ed. Wolff's humor also carries us through the painstaking hours before the prom as Nick politely tolerates his parents' reminiscences about their dating and silently appreciates his father's help in donning the tuxedo. Suspense rises along with Nick's nervous musings. Like most high school students, he is embarrassed that his mother drives him to the prom to meet Shana, but he reminds himself that there are lots of Special Ed kids who never even attended a prom. Shana hasn't arrived and he is getting cold outside the hotel where the prom will take place.

When chapter 4 begins with Nick still fighting off the cold outside the hotel, we know that something awful has happened. Nick is trying to be optimistic. Her parents must have had a flat tire. He dances to keep warm, thinks up math problems, and imagines the conversations he will have with Shana when she finally arrives. Finally he is beginning to work up an undirected anger, when he overhears a conversation between two adult chaperones about Special Ed. "No son of mine's gonna sit with the droolers. . . . You put a kid with the droolers, he'll end up a drooler" (65).

The anger is punched out of him. Still denying much of his hurt, he runs around the students as they leave, and makes his way to his father's car. Once he gets home, he runs past the questions of his parents, and up to his room where he tries to distract his mind by studying amphibians. Of course it doesn't work. His father makes a phone call and confirms the fact that Shana has lied to her parents, telling them that Nick had called her and cancelled their date. She has played a dirty trick. Nick decides it is because he is Special Ed and now that Shana has "gone Up," she considers him an embarrassing impediment to her social progress. Nick decides that her failure to show up means that he is stuck in Special Ed forever. In contrast to Shana, he won't "go anywhere" (76).

And now we suffer Nick's dream, in slow motion, as he and his sister Dianne beg their parents to come swimming, after a morning of riding ponies. Their parents laugh and promise "In a minute. In a minute" (79). Nick and Dianne run around the house to the pool, where Dianne jumps in and shows Nick how to tread water until she suddenly sinks, and Nick is watching only her bubbles. He can't get his parents there fast enough. Wolff makes us feel how trapped Nick is in this slow dream where his slowness is the reason for the death of his sister. This feeling is braided in with memories of his parents accepting the diagnosis of reading specialists that he needs Special Education. In Nick's mind, they seem to suspect that perhaps his learning disability is part of the cause of their daughter's death. Nick infers that his slowness in getting help is the whole reason Dianne has died. This chapter is painful to read, as Wolff's language mimics Nick's recollected realization of Dianne's death, his anger, and then the heavy, endless weight of guilt.

Now this traumatic memory is coupled with Shana's rejection of him. After his parents leave for work, Nick drinks whiskey, too much whiskey. Inevitably, he gets sick, and, like the nice boy he is, he cleans up after himself. This effort doesn't make him feel better about himself. Again, Wolff's humor keeps this sequence from becoming a sermon. Nick's simplistic candor in describing his thoughts and actions provides us a sort of Chaplinesque view of this drunken episode and, in parts, of his life. This remarkable sequence, however, is anything but simplistic and completely unfiltered by any irony on the character's part; it lets the reader see clearly into Nick's mind. It is an effective dramatic technique to trace Nick's growth.

And he does grow. From the malleable young man who followed the rules around him without trusting his own judgments, he is developing into someone who asserts his opinions, increasingly making choices about how to run his own life. At first, as with his escape into alcohol, his judgments are overblown and his choices awkward. Like many young teens who have been wronged, he indulges in a maudlin streak. Remembering how, six years ago, he had picked his dog Patsy from the others in the pound, he decides to think of himself not as the savior of his pet, but as the guilty murderer of all those he hadn't adopted. He refuses to go to school, and his parents, unaccustomed to such decisiveness, let him stay home, until Patsy has an accident.

Finally, Nick is working constructively on his project when he hears the yelp of a hurt animal; Patsy has been struck by a hit-and-run car. Focusing on how to get help for Patsy as quickly as possible, Nick makes decisions that seem right to him at the time, but could have been dangerous. He chooses to drive his mother's car without the requisite training to operate the clutch along with the brake. A slight accident causes an uproar, including a verbal Keystone-Kop routine in which one of the two police officers keeps on reiterating the name with which Nick has first identified himself—Special Ed—mistaking "Ed" for his given name. But Nick is more than "special" or "learning disabled." After all, he has managed to drive safely for most of the way, and was waylaid through no fault of his own. Most of his decisions have been good and solid, based on common sense and concern for his dog.

After Nick is safely ensconced at home with his parents, he realizes that their anger at his rash—though ultimately successful—actions epitomizes the ultimate fear of all parents, that their children will be hurt, or suffer, or worse, disappear or die. Suddenly Nick can see them with love, as people who also need reassurance that he won't leave them alone, as did his sister. Why did it happen? Who let Patsy out of the house? Nobody will ever know for sure.

Nick is growing beyond the assumption that the world runs according to stringent rules which some people understand better than others. Yes, there are codes and rules that make decisions easier and that keep people safe. Yes, there are patterns and events that are more likely to occur than others. On the other hand, life is more complicated than a mere collection of precepts and codes. There is a fluctuating rhythm to living that makes "probably" a more accurate term than "definitely."

Many people prefer certitude. When Nick's confidence in Shana is first jiggled by the note that drops from her notebook, Nick reassures himself that "there was no problem, probably" (26). However, that "probably" is worrisome; before he can calm down, Nick has to remember that "probably" also protects him from disasters like more bombs dropped on Japan and quiz failures. Nick becomes frustrated when the logic of "probably" won't allow him to wallow in his melancholy when he is thinking about his role in the adoption of Patsy (97). In the end, Nick realizes that living with "probably" is inevitable if he is going to live fully. Maturity means accepting that the complexity of life can result in moments of beauty as well as times of agonizing self-doubt.

Wolff incorporates several lessons in how to achieve at least a modicum of that maturity, but without the blatant didacticism that has historically pervaded much of the literature written for young people. Wolff believes that resilient people recognize the inevitability of pain in life and face it with directness and honesty. Finding and developing a passion in some craft or body of knowledge outside oneself can provide both an immediate escape and hope for a long-term alternative to the loneliness and helplessness of most painful situations. Finally, persistent pushing, that process of rising again and again from hardship, can blossom into achievements of exquisite beauty and the reward of self-esteem.

The doctor who bandages Nick's arm after Patsy's accident tells him that it is normal to feel hurt when people treat you unkindly. "Everybody's doing it. It's not fun, but it's necessary" (119). She speaks with evident authority; she herself was born with an eye so badly crossed that it seems to stare at the side of her nose. Yet, with goggles on, she looks the glamorous adventurer she is, who has climbed to the top of Mt. Hood and soon plans to try Mt. Rainier. She knows about learning that one path is impossible, and struggling until she finds another.

As with Dr. Willis's fascination with mountain climbing, and his mother's abiding interest in Beethoven, Nick has turned to the study of amphibians. This is his area of expertise, where he shines even among the "regular" kids. It is also what he does to keep him from thinking too much about what he perceives are his failures—academic, social, and personal. Nick also runs track; he isn't particularly fast, but he has endurance. He persists. That quality lets the violets in the track keep blooming, and it keeps Shana trying to explain her actions to Nick, even as he is running away from her. His perseverance, even when the situation seems impossible, is part stubbornness and part hope for a happier circumstance. It is mostly hope.

His persistence is rewarded by gradual improvement in his relations with others. Nick gets encouragement from Mr. Norton, his teacher, who cares enough to note his courage while paying him the respect it takes to punish him for disturbing the classroom. Nick's parents, particularly his father, support him with honest admiration and obvious affection. His friends in school are happy to see him return. Best of all, Shana has risked the certain anger of her parents and the penalty of an increased number of chores in order to spend time with him and to rebuild a relationship. For all of Nick's perceived insecurities, he is more fortunate than many high school students.

Shana tells Nick that she and another student, with the help of Mr. Norton, have determined that he might have "minimal brain dysfunction," a condition in which the connections among brain cells are irregular enough to cause difficulty in learning to read or in remembering. Nick is relieved that his problems have a name, that they are real. Shana also informs him that he is a "savant" because he is such an expert on amphibians. Nick has also succeeded at other science projects. Perhaps his expertise is a result of his persistent study of amphibians rather than any particular brain configuration; perhaps, as Shana suggests, his fascination derives from his sister's drowning. If Dianne had possessed the attributes of an amphibian, she would have been able to breathe underwater. Although Wolff does not indicate this possibility in any explicit way, a skeptical reader could infer that many of Nick's learning difficulties might arise from the emotional shock he underwent when his beloved older sister drowned. At the end of the book, Nick is beginning to make connections to his past experiences, some of which hurt to remember, but are invaluable in helping him to analyze his own nature and talents.

In the character of Nick, Wolff depicts a painful reality that most readers have experienced, that of feeling isolated on the margins of a social whirl, real or imagined. In an interview, she says, "I have so often felt like a parenthesis. Everything else in the world seems sure and I'm not. And I know kids feel that way. I know adolescents very often feel, 'I'm the only one in the class who doesn't get it or isn't being asked to the prom.' To feel like a parenthesis is a very common thing. The fact is that I happen to feel it and I'm past sixty" (Colburn, 3).

In some ways Wolff's first young adult novel is reminiscent of Salinger's *Catcher in the Rye*, one of the books she credits with inspiring her writing career, a book often designated as the first major young adult novel in American literature. In the story of Holden Caulfield, as in that of Nick Swansen, the young protagonist speaks his mind directly to the reader. Each takes the literal point of view of young teens emerging from the inexperience of childhood and the innocent assumption that people should know how to act with kindness and honesty. From the beginning, that innocence assures the reader that both will turn out all right. The reader hears the rhythm of many uncomfortable adolescent minds that bend in one direction one minute and then the opposite a minute later, between self-confidence and self-doubt, between affectionate appreciation for family and, a moment later, scorn and disdain for those same people.

This bifocal vision, taking in both the faults of the current situation and an idealized vision of a possible future, is typical of intelligent adolescents. They are emerging from a childhood where they have merely followed the path before them, usually prescribed by adults. Now they are beginning to face situations in which they must make choices. Neither Holden nor Nick feels capable of making responsible choices and yet neither wants to have all his choices made for him any longer. Middle-class teens live many years in this twilight between childhood and economic and social independence, swerving between autonomy and obedience.

Both of these hypersensitive young protagonists assume that society is driven by rules, and that some people are better at following them than others. Both are learning to live with many "shoulds" in their lives, yet they differ in what they value. While Holden is repulsed by the phoniness he sees in the sophisticated upper-middle-class society of New York and attracted to the simple, naïve loyalty of juveniles, Nick is emerging from a life of simplified loyalty to the rules of his teachers and parents and is attracted to the possibility of more sophisticated awareness. In some ways he is attracted toward the social games that Holden calls phony because they are the rituals that could identify him with the "regular" students; he wants to join in the games that seem to connect people in a social web. Nick makes his decision to ask Shana to the prom because he realizes that, although nobody from the Special Ed class has ever done so, there is no rule against going to the prom. While he is learning to dance in his room, he finds he even has to make his own rule to keep from stumbling over his dog, Patsy: No Dog Dancing (23).

For a while Nick does become a member of the social hierarchy, just by participating in the activities leading up to the prom. A varsity shortstop slings an arm over his shoulders as he is buying tickets for the boat ride after the prom: "a varsity arm around you isn't just an arm, and everybody knows it" (25). Just going through the same motions, just opening his mouth and responding, seems enough to make him belong. The main rule he must obey is not to be afraid. People "acted as if fear was something you shouldn't get, like dirty or drunk" (49). People are attracted to the appearance of confidence, even if it is just a matter of acting. Nick wonders if his sister had gotten scared toward the end of her drowning.

Both Nick and Holden seem mentally blocked by guilt over the death of a younger sibling. When Holden was thirteen, four years before the novel unfolds, his brother Allie died of leukemia; immediately afterward, Holden broke his hand in a rampage of frustration because he wasn't able to save him. Holden reminisces often about his brother Allie's sweetness, and wishes he had been nicer to him. If only Allie had lived, Holden thinks, life would have been more authentic.

Nick was younger than Holden, only five years old, when he watched his ten-year-old sister Dianne drown in a swimming pool. Confused and dazed, Nick feels that his slowness at getting help prevented her life from being saved. What Nick remembers is his sister's quick intelligence and her ability to ask and answer questions he could hardly articulate. Perhaps, he thinks, Dianne could have kept him from making mistakes. Perhaps she could have helped him understand girls.

Holden finally reaches out to his youngest sister Phoebe. As his trust in the possibility of goodness is deteriorating, he finds strength in Phoebe, who won't let him push her away. Despite all the insulting words that siblings tend to shower on each other, she shows authentic caring for Holden, and draws him home, where he needs to be. For Nick, his dog, Patsy, gives him similar comfort, asking no questions and making no judgments or demands. It is Nick's concern for Patsy that draws him out of his torpor after Shana's rejection. In rescuing Patsy, Nick takes risks and makes decisions. After their initial fear-induced anger, his parents begin to realize that Nick is more capable than a young boy and perhaps not as disabled as they had assumed. They begin to demand that he do more for himself and come out of himself. And this is where he needs to be.

Holden's contempt for the world is inverted by Nick into an underlying contempt for himself. Frustrated by the vagueness of his knowledge about dating—even what to ask about it, he berates himself: "What do you mean, Nick? Inside his brain was a terrible asking voice, almost yelling at him: What do you *mean?*" (27). Like Holden, he believes that life has a clarity visible to others that he just cannot see.

In other ways, however, their reactions are contrary. Holden feels that he alone recognizes authenticity; he is tremendously judgmental about the others he meets, and continually disappointed. In contrast, Nick is judgmental toward himself; he is only beginning to feel assured that he knows what he means when he talks to himself. While Nick is beginning to welcome more possibilities of relationships into his life, Holden is finding that one after another of his relationships are unsatisfactory; his options are narrowing.

The contrast between the voices of Holden Caulfield and Nick Swansen highlights their differences as characters. Holden is self-conscious about his public persona, addressing the reader directly as if he is convincing readers that they would share the same view if only they were there, using phrases like "You probably heard of it" (Salinger, *Catcher in the Rye*, 4) in referring to his prep school and "You should have seen him" (Salinger, 165) in describing an acquaintance he considers particularly phony. Like many teens, to confirm the truth of what he says he peppers his speech with sentences like "I'm not kidding" and "She really does." His speech urges listeners or readers to see what he sees and accept his sincerity. Part of the charm of Holden's voice in *The Catcher in the Rye* is that urgent longing to be understood by the reader; reading the book feels like listening to Holden explain himself, providing the sense that he deeply cares that we understand.

While Salinger writes using the first-person point of view to provide a sense of immediacy to the reader, Wolff uses the third-person point of view attached to Nick's mind (personal communication, March 2003). The voice of Nick is not only younger, more insecure and self-critical, but also more of a developing consciousness of self. It is directed more inward with little sense of an outside audience. It is cautious where Holden is reckless; it reserves judgments rather than making them. Although both he and Holden are sixteen, Nick still lives in a childhood world where he expects kindness from adults and protects himself from contact with his peers. He reaches out to others only after much forethought, and he is surprised when any of his spontaneous statements makes an impact. He never uses the slightly shocking scatology that is habitual for Holden.

Holden is in full explosion, scattering from impulse to action and then retrieving the pieces. He stubbornly runs into violence because he won't back off from what he considers the truth. His story is the process toward self-destruction, a process finally slowed by Phoebe's insistent intervention. Nick's story is that of a self-consciousness struggling slowly from buried memories and teenage urges into light, as he learns how to face situations directly and clearly. The reader is charmed by sharing Nick's inner voice as it emerges from childishness to incipient adulthood. It is unique because it articulates that change with the clarity of social innocence. Most people make this development so gradually that it is difficult to perceive; Nick's special situation gives the reader an opportunity to hear a voice familiar to us all. The vulnerability and self-doubt so universal to young people are magnified in Nick by his mental differences and by his family trauma. The poignancy of his experience triggers memories of similar painful losses. Wolff's clear and direct language makes it possible to share his journey imaginatively.

The Catcher in the Rye is as emotionally satisfying as sharing an intense experience with a close friend. *Probably Still Nick Swansen* is more subtle, reflecting the development of a more introverted character. Both share a directness of language which is reminiscent of attending an internal dramatic production. Wolff's deep interest in literary expression extends beyond her early poetry, short stories, and her writing of novels. From her childhood thrill of watching the musical production *Oklahoma* in New York City to her extensive experience with theater during her marriage to actor and director Art Wolff, she has been attracted to the direct expression of thought through speech, unadulterated with description. In addition to Salinger, one of the writers she has most admired is the playwright Arthur Miller, whom she met when she received the National Book Award in 2001 when he was being honored for his lifetime achievement.

Beginning with *Probably Still Nick Swansen,* Virginia Euwer Wolff's novels persistently focus on matching the style of her language with the personal development of her character. Her novels have become increasingly suitable for Reader's Theater, where a book is read aloud and readers dramatize the words of the characters. The author's disclaimer that she used "some incorrect grammar and punctuation in order to tell Nick Swansen's story in language that is consistent with his" (Author's Note) provides a clue that this novel is close to being a dramatic monologue, a story reported in the voice of a young boy in the process of defining himself, yet still only tentatively sure of his decisions.

How trustworthy are his ideas about himself? Whom can he trust? On the one hand, his sister had been his whole map for how to live, yet she disappeared with a suddenness that slashed his trust in himself. And Shana's failure to appear at the prom undercut the new sense of capability that he was beginning to develop. On the other hand, he has saved his dog's life, and has been able to accept Shana's apology. In school he is still pretty good at remembering facts about amphibians. To be or not to be. That is his question. The answer is probably affirmative. The intensity of his interior monologue demonstrates the truth of the passage Wolff quoted from Saul Bellow's *The Adventures of Augie March:*

> In yourself you labor, you wage and
> combat, settle scores, remember insults,
> fight . . . triumph, . . . cry, persist,
> die and rise again. All by yourself!
> Where is everybody? Inside your breast
> and skin, the entire cast.

The drama of Nick Swansen's life is within him, and to choose to be is to acknowledge all those characters within as valid and as worthy of existence as anybody else's drama. Some of those events and characters aren't the characters and events Nick would choose. Some cannot be controlled by Nick or his parents and teachers. But, like the sad anomaly of Beethoven's inability to hear the gorgeous music he was writing, some things must be. To accept what has seemed unbearable in the past and to press on with full engagement in whatever chances life offers is to set the stage for growth. At the end of the novel, Nick grudgingly decides that he is not completely willing to lose his tentative trust in the future, and he will not close down to depression and fear. Nick admits to himself that his life would "probably" continue and he "probably" would still be himself (175).

The ending of Salinger's novel is ambiguous. Neither we nor Holden himself are quite sure of his future. Yet what ending could be more appropriate for this novel and this protagonist with his awkward moment-by-moment quest to catch and hold on to meaning? Wolff's book shares the same type of ending, and it reflects her conviction that there is no guarantee of a happy ending to life; in fact, very little in life is completely dependable. Both endings are emotionally satisfying because they seem real; they mimic human relationships outside of fiction. Perhaps Wolff was so strongly influenced by Salinger's work because she shares the same worldview, deeply skeptical and realistic, yet steadfast in admiring innocence and hope. In this first young adult novel, Wolff is more cautious in expressing her cynicism; she will take more risks in future books.

Like Salinger, Virginia Euwer Wolff often creates images so precisely real that they remain in the reader's memory. In this book, one example occurs near the beginning, capturing Nick's dawning awareness of romantic possibilities with Shana: "the camera clicked with Nick's mouth wide open, as if he was eating sunshine" (14). Later in the book, after Shana has rejected him and he has returned to school, he feels "jagged, I've got jagged edges. Like a sawblade" (134) in a world of smoothly rounded people.

Probably Still Nick Swansen received critical recognition immediately after its publication in 1988, including the Booklist Editor's Choice, the *School Library Journal* Best Book of the Year, the International Reading Association Young Adult Book Award, and a YALSA Best Book for Young Adults. Since then, more readers are discovering its quiet charm. It has won the Children's Book Award for PEN (USA Center West) and was named one of YALSA's 100 Best of the Best Books for Young Adults from 1967–1992, and again in 1994, and a YALSA Popular Paperback for Young Adults in 1999. One reviewer praised Wolff's "thoughtful attention to original characterization" (*Kirkus Reviews*, 1991). In a starred review in the *School Library Journal*, it was called a "strong, compassionate story," an opinion which an increasing number of readers share, particularly in reference to the author's depiction of a character with minimal brain dysfunction.

Few other writers have been able to draw a character whose person-ality compels us to see him as so much more than the labeled disability. Like all but a few people with such specially labeled differences, Nick is memorable for his ideas and his experiences; his different pace of learning is a minor aspect of who he is and who he might become. In one of Wolff's favorite letters from students, a girl in California said that this was the first book she had ever finished reading. Wolff corre-sponded with her for several years until the girl developed beyond their initial relationship (Gallo, 6). With the sensitivity of a true teacher, Wolff let the correspondence go.

During the final stages of writing this novel, Wolff was feeling some-what disappointed about her own life; she had never owned a house nor had she fulfilled her dreams of traveling. While skiing, she broke her arm so badly that two surgeries were required. It was a tough year. But, like Nick, she struggled out of her own particular "slough of despond." Honored by a request from Roger Sutton to be interviewed for Chicago Public Radio, Wolff decided to quit a longtime habit of smoking. She worried that she could not sit through an interview without coughing. So she attended an intensive stop-smoking workshop where she learned about the characteristics of resilience and persistence. Some of these les-sons reflected what she already knew and had incorporated in *Probably Still Nick Swansen*. A similar wisdom informs the characters in *The Mozart Season* and the *Make Lemonade* series who, like Nick, struggle against circumstances that seem impossibly daunting.

References

Colburn, Nell. "The Incomparable Wolff," *School Library Journal* 48, no. 2 (February 2002).

Gallo, Don. "Virginia Euwer Wolff." Authors4Teens.com, http://www.authors4teens.com/A4T?source=interview&authorid=wolff (16 Jan. 2001).

Salinger, J. D. *The Catcher in the Rye.* Boston: Little, Brown, and Co., 1945, 1951.

Sutton, Roger. "An Interview with Virginia Euwer Wolff," *The Horn Book* 77, no. 3 (May/June 2001).

Wolff, Virginia. "If I Was Doing It Proper, What Was You Laughing At?" *The Horn Book 74*, no.3 (May 1998: 297–308).

Zvirin, Stephanie. "The Booklist Interview: Virginia Euwer Wolff," *Booklist* (1 Mar. 1994).

CHAPTER 3

~

The Mozart Season:
The Gifts of Music

Like many writers and other artists who spend so much energy and time working toward understanding the relationship of suffering and joy, Virginia Euwer Wolff lives seriously. For Wolff, playing the violin is what keeps her both connected to and balanced between the pain and joy that is life. In interviews she has intimated that music pulls her away from that gray feeling of malaise when nothing seems to matter and life seems a mere joke. Toward the other extreme, when pain seems unbearable, music rounds out those sharp pangs so they can bubble up and safely dissolve.

Wolff began learning music at age seven, studying the piano for one year before beginning violin lessons at age eight. Except for a fifteen-year hiatus after college, she has performed in orchestras since she was ten. Music influences her writing and her life "every day, all day" (Colburn, 56). She began violin lessons at age eight, changing over from piano lessons, partly because she was attracted to the glamour of the violin, particularly after she heard a cousin play during a trip to New York. The gorgeous color of the polished woods, their sinuous shape, the sweep of the bows as they arc over the instrument held high in the air, and, of course, the exquisite variety of the sounds it produces—all these have mesmerized and moved her all her life since.

Music and the violin also seemed to keep her bound to at least a tenuous thread of reason after the shattering experience of her father's death when she was five. She continued her violin lessons until she finished college. She married, moved frequently, began rearing children, and ignored her instrument for about fifteen years. Then, she writes, "haltingly, as I've done most things in my life," she began playing again; at age fifty, after thirty years, she began taking lessons again. "It was one of the most humbling, horrifying, and ultimately rewarding experiences I've ever had," she writes (Colburn, 56).

Now that she has retired from teaching school, she spends much of her time practicing music, playing music with friends, and participating in musical performances. Many days, she begins playing her violin in the mornings even before she writes. *The Mozart Season*, which explores how music can connect the joy and pain of people, is dedicated to her parents, Florence Craven Euwer and Eugene Courtney Euwer, "who gave me music."

Wolff's keen urge to match sound and rhythm with meaning pervades her published writing. In her fictionalized autobiographical novel, *Rated PG*, music streams through the summer Wolff describes, when protagonist Bitsy "comes of age" at sixteen, discovers the joy of learning new books, new language, and new courage under the guidance of a twenty-year-old boy, before she is sent to boarding school by her mother. In *Rated PG*, Bitsy takes violin lessons from a German teacher from Salzburg, Mr. Seligman, who had lost two daughters under the Nazi regime. She is studying Mozart's Fourth Concerto, and trying to decide the appropriate length and touch of a fermata. Musical references flow through her mind, resonating with her fluctuating adolescent moods, and, to her readers who are musically educated, acting as ready metaphors for her emotional states. In Wolff's first novel for young adults, *Probably Nick Swansen*, allusions to Beethoven characterize his mother as a music lover, and remind Nick that struggling with crises can result in a depth of understanding or expression that can be quite beautiful. The format of a later novel, *Bat 6*, will reflect her experience with various musical groups where separate unique voices interweave to create a coherent expression different from any single strand of sound or meaning. Her most recent works, *Make Lemonade* and *True Believer*, make music out of words as Wolff uses a new format to arrange the narrator's language in lines that reflect the length of each thought or utterance. Combining her love of drama, her musical experiences, and her sensitivity toward the nuances of language, she creates a piece where sound and sense merge appropriately to portray a unique character and her story. *Make Lemonade* introduces the main characters and sets the scenery and the mood. *True Believer* tells a more mature story of an older character; its overall tone is more somber though it ultimately ends with a deeper joy. While *The Mozart Season* explores issues related to music, Wolff's later work moves toward a more conscious melding of music with language.

The Mozart Season was inspired by Wolff's musings at an outdoor concert in Portland, Oregon. She noticed one of the girls who was turning the pages for a performer, and began wondering about her life. What was her relationship to music? How did she know the performer? What else did she do? What moved and motivated her? The answers to these questions became the protagonist of *The Mozart Season*, Allegra, a twelve-year-old violinist whose father and mother are classical musicians and whose similar devotion to music does not keep her from playing softball in the spring.

Allegra Leah Shapiro is a completely different character from Wolff's previous characters. After writing about the learning difficulties of Nick in *Probably Nick Swansen*, Wolff wanted to write about a character for whom learning was easy. In an essay for *The Horn Book* in 1998, Wolff compares various uses of language to define various communities, especially to delineate insiders from outsiders. Nick struggles to understand how the world in which he lives works by listening to the words of others. He barely trusts his own perceptions, and he has trouble expressing his own views so that they can be understood. He feels like a square peg in a round hole, and his parents and many of his peers perceive him that way. It is an uncomfortable fit. Wolff describes Allegra: In contrast to Nick, "here is a girl who fits in her community so comfortably, whose support system is so clear and stable that she's free to pursue excellence. And that was what I was interested in [*The Mozart Season*]" (305–6).

Allegra has just finished the sixth grade and a successful softball season in which she made a catch that helped the team win a crucial game. Now she is preparing to enjoy a summer that is chock-full of creative enterprise—making a vocabulary list, cuddling her cat Heavenly Days, and resuming her violin lessons with Mr. Kaplan in full force. Allegra is surrounded by people who care deeply about her, who have the wisdom and goodwill to provide what is good for her development as a whole person, rather than as a badge of achievement. Mr. Kaplan, her violin teacher, shows his support for her, not through empty praise, but through careful listening and honest appraisal, making her think long and hard to form responses to his questions. Allegra and her two girlfriends, Jessica and Sarah, tacitly agree to treat each other with kindness, avoiding sensitive subjects and appreciating each other's differences rather than making fun of them. So close are they during the year in school, and so unique are their interests that their teachers affectionately call them the "Three Weird Sisters" (129), after the three witches who chant together in Shakespeare's *Macbeth*. Allegra's parents are both musical; her father is a university teacher who plays the cello and teaches music theory classes, and her mother plays the violin for the Oregon Symphony. Busy, involved in meeting their performance deadlines and fostering their friendships, they insist on making time for a nightly family dinner. Still, they tend to be as tightly wound and as easily worried as most parents of adolescents. Brother David, a sixteen-year-old talented cartoonist, has a mordant outlook on the foibles of American middle-class life that balances the seriousness of his parents and his sister. He generously mentors his sister, offering an unusually mature perspective on the questions that arise during this summer of surprising discoveries.

Allegra is going to need this strong web of support. During her first lesson of the summer, Mr. Kaplan reminds her of the audiotape they had made the previous February of her playing Mozart's Fourth Concerto in D as a submission to the Ernest Bloch Competition for young musicians of Oregon. Mr. Kaplan informs Allegra that she has been selected as one of six finalists. It is quite an honor for such a young girl to be chosen from over eighty entrants, but it will mean devoting her summer to practicing Mozart and, worse, in Allegra's mind, performing the whole concerto in public. However, she decides that she will undertake the challenge, almost on a whim as an impulsive response to a photo of a handsome young man, a musical prodigy, that she sees in her music teacher's studio. Fortunately, Allegra's nature is not usually whimsical, for her choice will cause a deep lasting impact; her summer with Mozart will take her beyond the emotional and mental boundaries that normal young girls of twelve want even to approach. She will learn more about music than a class could teach and, most likely, more about herself than she can imagine.

In the process, she will also develop from a young girl into a young adult, sharing adult knowledge with her family and participating in responsibilities. Informed by new information and her summer experience, she will even begin to enjoy a real romantic episode, not based on a whimsical attraction to an image in a photo.

Her first task of the summer is to memorize the concerto, practicing the sequence of notes so well that she can play them automatically, without thinking, like climbing stairs. First she looks at the overall shape of the piece, then plays it all the way through, and then practices the difficult parts thousands of times. It's important that the mental path be so well worn that she can focus on artistic aspects other than the mechanics. Wolff, in the persona of Allegra, makes an analogy to skiing, where getting to the end of the run is so consuming that your mind has to stay right where your body is. It takes an almost maniacal drive to master the skills necessary to play Mozart well enough to reach this stage.

Memorizing and practicing the technical parts of the music are barely half the process. Mr. Kaplan instructs her to get as close to Mozart as possible, even though there are numerous obstacles. "There are more than two hundred years. And there's all that ocean. And his mind and your mind" (47). Allegra labels this process "Closing the Distance" and courageously devotes herself to the long process. She listens to different recordings, she practices, and she agrees to fill in for another young soloist who has broken her fingers windsurfing. This is the first time Allegra will play all three movements in public with an orchestra accompanying her. Even though the orchestra is an amateur group in a small town about seventy miles east of Portland, Allegra is quite fearful of the responsibility of playing a solo in front of an orchestra. She senses the loyalty that the orchestra feels to Karen Coleman, the nineteen-year-old college girl who has broken her fingers. She imagines her to be a sharply attractive expert, tall and poised, wearing stage makeup. The rehearsal leaves her fearful and exhausted, especially as she is struggling with jealousy, sparked by overhearing a conversation comparing her with Karen.

However, as she played the solo, she had become so intensely involved in the music that she forgot where she was. She had overcome her self-consciousness and moved into a zone of inspiration.

Her teacher is pleased; she has become so familiar with the muscular movements and emotional responses necessary to play Mozart com-

Wolff draws on her experiences with music to enrich her writing.

petently that she is almost at the point where she is close enough to embrace him, but this is not easy. In fact, Mr. Kaplan acknowledges "how difficult it is to do the perfectly natural thing" and describes a violinist who claimed he played a whole movement while asleep on stage (125). On the one hand, Allegra should lose her self-consciousness almost to the point of sleep. On the other hand Mr. Kaplan urges her to assert herself more uniquely into the performance. She is supposed to remember "ME: Allegra Shapiro—I'M playing this concerto" (126). So, Allegra spends hours of intense energy practicing and playing and even thinking about the piece, until her brother David accuses her of approaching craziness.

At the same time that Allegra is in the process of naturalizing herself to the Fourth Concerto, she is also in the process of developing from an elementary school child into a young adult. She is also learning to assert herself within her family. She insists that her family really listen to her with the same intensity that they listen to adults. At first, when she is trying to attract her father's attention to her news about the Bloch Competition, she feels like a child, whining "Daddy, this is important!" (18). Later, when her mother fails to respond to what she has said, she merely repeats herself. This is a first step toward her parents beginning to consider her input as relevant to their decisions about her life.

At the beginning of the novel, both parents are trying with all their might to let Allegra have complete independence in making the decision about whether or not to enter the Bloch Competition. Although both hold their breath while she asks for their opinions, they wisely decide that only Allegra can know whether she has the will to devote herself wholly to Mozart for the entire summer. When she makes that decision, they show her proper respect as a professional; they include her equally on a sign-up sheet for practicing time in the music room. Her father also asks if she will act as a paid page-turner during a concert, and then, after her success, her mother relays requests from her professional colleagues for more jobs. Neither parent ever recommends that she practice more, nor do they ever offer advice about her music. They seem to bend over backwards not to be the kind of parents who push their children to succeed for their own gratification. Both love music and both delight in the successes of their musical daughter, but no more or less than in the successes of their cartoonist son.

At first Allegra is angry at her parents for not informing her immediately that she was a Bloch Competition finalist. She feels left out of a secret that she was the last person to know. Why hadn't they told her sooner? Mr. Kaplan explains that he wanted her to learn the piece without the shadow of competition clouding her relationship with the music: "I want you first to love the music. *Then* compete" (49). Wolff is exploring the nature of information shared and withheld, especially between young people and adults. When are secrets appropriate?

Allegra manifests her budding independence in a most responsible fashion, as she exercises her tendency for compassion for two troubled adults. One is Deirdre, a dear friend of her mother's who is staying with the family while she performs in the city. Deirdre is highly emotional, intensely warm one minute, quivering with nervous energies the next. She is obviously a needy person, even with all of her musical successes. The other is also a member of the musical world, albeit only on the margins. As Allegra begins to attend more outdoor concerts, she notices a figure who sparks her curiosity. The Dancing Man is ragged and obviously poor, but his face lights up when the music starts and he moves rhythmically in a sort of dance as long as the music plays. Right after the concert, he seems to disappear. Allegra is drawn to him by the rapt delight in his face, but also puzzled. How can such joy exist in a man who is obviously poor and alone? As Allegra inserts herself into the lives of these two people, motivated by pity and curiosity at first, she finds herself more capable of helping than she would have imagined.

Deirdre arrives, with all her glamorous intensity. Although Allegra has always been aware of a secret in her past, her curiosity peaks when she sees this elegant soloist who has taught her such profound lessons about the nature of music melt into hysteria when an earring falls into her father's cello. This is not such a terribly big deal to most people. Obviously Deirdre is quite fragile, but nobody tells Allegra why, so she just accepts it. Neither does Allegra tell her parents that she has begun to unwind from the stresses of Mozart by bike riding in the park in the middle of the night. Her parents are shocked, almost to disbelief, when a neighbor reports seeing her. They become livid, angry in their terrible fear for her. In turn, Allegra is frustrated. "I'm supposed to be a child . . . and I'm supposed to be an adult and be responsible. How can I be

everything at the same time?" (145). After their outburst, they explain
Deirdre's pain and, at the same time, share the reasons for their own
terror.

Like all mature parents, they live in horrible dread of losing the children they love almost more than life itself. Because they are asking Allegra to participate in adult responsibilities, they are now sharing adult
knowledge with her. "Suffering and joy. That's all there is. There isn't
anything else" (152), explains Allegra's father. Some people may live
halfheartedly, where nothing is serious and everything seems a joke.
However, to experience the intense joy of life's beautiful possibilities,
suffering its awful agonies and bleak drudgeries is also necessary. All of
Wolff's stories include characters whose lives matter because they
stretch to include both joy and sorrow. Her young people face adult situations with the resiliency of youthful willingness to become aware of
horrible pain. Allegra is about to learn perhaps the most adult information that she will ever hear, but not from her parents. She is about
to learn about how deeply guilt can humiliate a person, grinding a spirit
into mud, and then, conversely, how to use that guilt to create joy. Her
friend Jessica tells her that the Chinese use bamboo as a symbol of
bending without breaking (142), like the Dancing Man who dances
even in the midst of his troubles, and like Beethoven who composed in
the midst of his illnesses, as described in *Probably Nick Swansen*. First,
Mr. Kaplan tells her that she is almost upstaging Mozart. "You are almost on top of him" (163). Allegra has just run through the concerto
automatically, with no mistakes; she is feeling good, as if she has just
run a good race or skied down a run with no glitches. However, Mr. Kaplan expresses concern: "Great music isn't something we master; it's
something we try all our lives to merge with" (166). Now it is Allegra
who wilts in shame at focusing only on her own skills without giving
herself to the music. Her respect for the genius of Mozart is so profound
that she is mortified to think that she might have forgotten to respect
the music as she played it. Feeling humiliated, however, will not bring
her closer to the music; she must find a way to convey the spirit of the
concerto as well as its technical brilliance.

Mr. Kaplan points the way when he asks Allegra to play the Brahms
Lullaby, a technically simple piece that most violin students learn very
soon. Closing her eyes, she sees a whimpering baby in a shabby room,

lying in a box, and lets her body play the piece; the result is exquisite. She needs to practice one of the techniques Deirdre has suggested: "You have to remember everything you've ever learned, and simultaneously forget all of it and do something totally new" (58). Forgetting that self-conscious anxiety lets you make the music your own. Now that Allegra has practiced and practiced the piece to the point that she is able to remember where every muscle should move, she needs to find a way to take her mind away from that self-consciousness at the same time.

Soon after her discouraging lesson with Mr. Kaplan, Allegra receives a package from her grandmother, her father's mother, who lives in New York City. Bubbe Raisa was born in Poland in 1921; she was thirteen before she saw the black armbands that the Nazis made all Jews wear to identify them as undesirable. At thirteen she didn't understand their implication and missed the irony of her father's naming them tribal symbols. In 1939, when she was eighteen, her parents sent her away to stay with relatives in New York City. She never saw them again, and later investigations indicated that they died in the death camp at Treblinka. Only later did Allegra's grandmother realize the significance of the cloth purse that her mother had tucked into her luggage. She knew she was most likely saying a final good-bye to the only daughter she had left. The purse she had embroidered as a child and displayed with pride in a photo of her along with the geese she shepherded symbolizes the connection between her past and her daughter's new life in America.

Now Bubbe Raisa is sending that same purse, which she has kept framed under glass in her home all her life, to Allegra. She is sending it because Allegra's middle name, Leah, honors the girl in the photo, and because Allegra's eyes show the same tenderness of hope and imagination (169).

As Allegra looks at the gift, she feels first a terrible sense of inadequacy. She is fully aware of how much Bubbe Raisa wants to embrace her fully within the Jewish faith. But Allegra is only half-Jewish; how can she live up to the responsibility of this gift? She feels encumbered, both by the purse and by Mozart. Why is she putting herself through all this? Will she go a little mad, just as Deirdre has when she reacted with such utter panic to dropping her earring in Mr. Shapiro's cello? Allegra becomes angry at all the suffering in the world and at the people who inflict it upon others. She is angry until her friends help her realize that she can help alleviate some of the world's pain. Now she decides that she will devote her performance of the concerto that has enveloped her summer to the memory of her namesake, Leah, the mother of Bubbe Raisa. This is what she can do, even if it seems useless. When she tells her grandmother what she intends, Bubbe Raisa gives her vow a name; playing the concerto while thinking about Leah will be her way of saying Kaddish, a Jewish prayer of the dead that honors by remembering.

Allegra asks her grandmother to keep this conversation private, only between the two of them. Bubbe Raisa invites her to New York, and promises to tell her the "stories of who you are" (193). This will be a part of Allegra that is separate from her parents. Allegra is developing into an individual, fed by her personal experiences with Mozart and Mr. Kaplan, the music she has made in the park with Deirdre, and her conversations with her friends. Like her parents, she will choose when and what to share. At the end of the book, Allegra's mother demonstrates her trust in her daughter by granting her permission to visit Bubbe Raisa and Deirdre in New York City. The Mozart season has earned Allegra the respect of her parents. She is a young adult.

Although very much based on Wolff's knowledge of music and musicians, *The Mozart Season* is not particularly the story of her own experiences as a musician. Her own musical talent did not develop as quickly as Allegra's, and her family was not professionally involved in music. However, the musical piece that is the focus of the book, Mozart's Violin Concerto No. 4, is a work that Wolff regretted having failed to conquer as a teen. In featuring this concerto as Allegra's challenge, Wolff perhaps exorcises a leftover feeling of disappointment for not having fully developing her own version ("Interview," 2).

From 1773 to 1775, Mozart wrote five violin concertos, all before he reached the age of twenty, just as the American Revolution was brewing in this country. At the time he lived in Salzburg, and most likely composed them for either himself or the lead soloist of the Salzburg court orchestra. Mozart reported to his father that he had played the Concerto in D Major. "It flowed like oil; everyone praised the beautiful, pure tone" (Donat, 6). The first of the three movements opens with a marching rhythm, very regular, definite, and sprightly. The second movement, in A major, slows down to a lyrical sequence with a wistful air; it ends tentatively, with little sense of resolution and with a feeling of still wanting something, a sort of subtle yearning. The final movement, like the middle, begins slowly but then quickens into a dance, though more dignified than cheerful. The exquisite joy of the violin as it soars is tinged with sadness, as if remembering pain. The best way, perhaps the only way, to understand this concerto that lived with Allegra all summer is to listen to it played by someone who understands the connection of joy and pain that Wolff is describing. As Mr. Kaplan admits, "Talking about music is like dancing about architecture" (50).

Besides the page-turner who inspired the character of Allegra, Wolff included another figure from her own life, a man whom she had seen at several concerts, dancing alone. At the concerts that Allegra attends, she notices a shabbily dressed man who dances alone to the music he hears in his head as well as what the concert plays. As first her mother's opera singer friend Deirdre and then her own friends choose to join the man in his dance, Allegra learns that Mr. Trouble, as he calls himself, expresses his thoughts with limited language, probably because of mental retardation from eating lead paint as a child. Gentle and earnestly inspired by the concerts, he vaguely remembers a melody which he calls "Waltz Tree." Allegra decides to search for the lost melody; she understands how nameless music can run through the mind, creating a yearning for the forgotten connection of sound and label. She searches unsuccessfully through music books, the Internet, and through sources at the library. Finally, at the last concert of the summer season, she sees the Dancing Man listening extra carefully as the orchestra is playing Sibelius's *Valse Triste*. The dramatic melancholy of this "sad waltz" touches a sympathetic chord within the shabby dancer called Trouble. Allegra compares him to a print hanging in the music room at her home, Marc Chagall's *The Green Violinist*. Music seems to flow through the Dancing Man as in Chagall's picture, in which the man's face is distorted so that his mouth looks like a chute, a place where thoughts might easily escape. The Dancing Man's life seems as scattered as the flying objects in the painting. Allegra is reassured to learn that the Dancing Man is being cared for by the Gospel Mission where he eats and sleeps and by the police who keep a watch over him. In Chagall's print, Allegra notices a small figure of a man with his arms out to catch the figures who are flying—an image reminiscent of Holden Caulfield's fantasy that underlies the title of Salinger's book, *The Catcher in the Rye*.

It is also an image of Mrs. Shapiro's relationship with her friend Deirdre, an immensely talented opera singer whose personal life keeps exploding. The two women had met at Juilliard, the internationally famous college for musicians. Allegra's mother, Fleur, had arrived there from Kansas, feeling as naïve as Dorothy in *The Wizard of Oz*. Deirdre, who seemed so glamorous by comparison, befriended her, and the two have maintained an intimate friendship ever since. Now it is Fleur who offers solace to Deirdre when her composure periodically shatters, as panic reduces her into a sobbing, shaking mass of tears. While Deirdre's career has soared, with reviews rating her singing at the level of genius, she herself has been traumatized by seeing her only daughter's life smashed into nothingness. A careless driver had let alcohol and drugs affect the discipline that would have prevented his car from careening over the young girl's body. Since then, the men Deirdre meets have treated her sensitivity with similar carelessness.

Allegra sees Deirdre crumble, and she also sees her mother soothe away the pain, so that Deirdre is able to function again. Allegra has learned that quality of compassion from her mother, and it has helped her lay her own claim on Mozart's music. While performing the Fourth Concerto during the competition, it is her deeply felt pity for her great-grandmother in Poland that defines the space between Mozart's notes and her own interpretation. It is how she can make Mozart's music her own.

"You're a person of empathy and drive and . . . courage" (245), pronounces Allegra's mother, at the end of this Mozart summer. Allegra has been able to embrace the music of Mozart because she has had the drive to master the techniques of playing, to memorize it both physically and mentally. She has had the empathy to comprehend the emotional aspect of Mozart, to play a "staggeringly soulful rendering, almost ethereal shaping of the . . . simultaneous whimsy and tragedy of the Mozartean vision" (232). Finally she has had the courage to pursue the painful knowledge of her great-grandmother's death at the Nazi death camp at Treblinka, to befriend and assist the shabby Dancing Man in search of his missing song, and to let herself imagine the persistent triumphs amid despair of Deirdre's life. As an incipient mature artist, as a young adult who is more than one of the "mall babies" (147), Allegra becomes capable of comprehending both the suffering and the joy of a life lived fully and deeply.

Pain connects the whole human species, says Allegra's mother, talking about how Deirdre, when she sings, "is giving her pain a voice, and . . . asking what it means" (244). Developing empathy is the method for opening the lines of connection. Why does pain, rather than joy, specially connect people? Perhaps it is because pain is particular, each person's suffering is uniquely qualified and felt, whereas joy is ethereally general, like the angelic togetherness in Dante's Paradise. Suffering is privately felt and internally retained, whereas authentic laughter is publicly released; it's catching.

The Mozart Season was a difficult book for Wolff to write, although she was able to draw on her many experiences as a violinist and as a participant in musical groups. The number of characters and stories surrounding the main character made it feel as if she "were holding one of those great big bouquets of balloons and had lost all their strings" (Zivrin, 1251). She succeeds, however, in weaving the complex plotlines into a thematic network with a number of subtle relationships. One value of this book is that it can inspire readers to see how talent builds on both the sheer ability to work hard and the personal sensitivity to interpret deeply. How much pain is necessary to make joy, and what is that process?

Another motif is the nature of friendship, and its importance as a stabilizing influence. Allegra's two closest friends, Jessica and Sarah, are similar to her in many ways. Both come from families with enough means to let the girls pursue their interests. Sarah is attending a ballet camp during the summer, luxuriating in the opportunity to work without interruption at the art she loves. She calls herself a Nutcracker Victim, because she became stricken with an obsessive love for dance after seeing a performance of this perennial favorite. Jessica, the daughter of a black geologist who has died and a Chinese woman, is visiting relatives in Hong Kong, where she continues her study of the Chinese language and customs. In an interview, Wolff explains her concept of the privileged life as it applies to these girls: "Privilege has nothing to do with fancy cars and cell phones and electronic gadgets and possessions. . . . But privilege has to do with enjoyment of beauty and the opportunity, the freedom, to enjoy beauty every single day. That's what I mean by a privileged life" (Colburn, 56). The friendship of these three girls centers on their mutual respect for each other's deep involvements in individual activities and the sense of responsibility and creativity that springs from that engagement. They listen to each other's stories and ask leading questions, but they don't insist on knowing everything about each other, nor do they pursue topics that might hurt. When Allegra feels discouraged after receiving the purse from Bubbe Raisa, Sarah and Jessica rally to her side and help her figure out how she will react. After Allegra's impressive performance in the competition, they help her celebrate. This is what good friends do; they share their lives, but they also let each other develop as individuals. Good friendships balance between freedom and interference. Good friends pay attention to what is trying to be said to help each other think out their options. Allegra's mother has that kind of relationship with her friend from college, Deirdre.

Wolff also describes the kinds of friendships that happen among musicians. Allegra's parents are obviously part of a large community of musicians with similar interests. They meet each other at concerts, playing together and listening to each other. Although Allegra, as a child who attends concerts with her family, has all her life been a marginal part of this community, now she is becoming more of an equal participant, beginning as a highly recommended page-turner. Allegra has friends of all ages who play with her in the Youth Orchestra, especially an older girl who has shared a music stand with her. Stand partners need to cooperate; since one turns the pages for both, they must communicate about how to manage the music. Lois, Allegra's former stand partner, called her "Little Buddy," and helped her with good humor and good advice. Unfortunately, she is moving away. But new acquaintances form quickly among musicians, and now Allegra learns that a highly talented musician might not also have the skills of friendship. When Deirdre visits, she tells Allegra about a boy she remembers as a toddler playing with Lego blocks. Now he has grown into a violinist of stunning talent and is moving to Portland. Steve Landauer will become Allegra's new stand partner.

Steve Landauer is Wolff's portrayal of a different type of player than Allegra. He is driven; he practices incessantly, even during the breaks at rehearsals when most other players stretch or talk. He fails to respond to ordinary gestures of friendliness, and seems insultingly aloof. Because Allegra is younger and has not garnered a reputation for playing, he discounts her. Music and the recognition he receives from performing are the way he measures his own self-worth. His father has married four times, and Steve Landauer has probably had little attention except for his artistic expertise. Playing music has become an escape from the strife of his family and from loneliness. If he doesn't achieve excellence at the skill he has chosen to define himself, he will feel like a blank, who will neither deserve nor get any notice from the people around him. He is less than a whole person. His ability to play Mozart's notes with expertise, with technical brilliance, is all he has to offer. When he eventually receives less than the top prize at the Bloch Competition, he is unable to respond to any mention of the contest with grace; he can only busy himself with trivial tasks and conversation. Steve Landauer's goal is to become a concert performer at Carnegie Hall, an acme of musical achievement in the United States. Anything less means failure to him. He lacks the healthy balance of Allegra and her family, who value friends, fellowship, and family memories as much as artistic achievement.

Steve's lack of warmth and grace is particularly evident in the scene when all the young contestants of the Bloch contest get stuck in an elevator, immediately after being interviewed by a talk show host who is clueless about music. Karen challenges Steve to join in the repartee. All the others are doing their best to help stem the panic that so naturally arises when people are confined to a small space with no definite respite in sight. Although these teens are in direct competition for a much coveted prize, they begin to share stories and to bond—all except Steve. He has never learned the give-and-take of light conversation among peers. When Karen insists on a response, he tries his best, and they reward him with appreciative applause. Wolff implies that those who live with good music are generally good people, who learn to cooperate, even in competitive situations. However, when asked whether characters like Steve Landauer actually exist, Wolff has indicated that they do.

Musical competition can be a strong motivation to spend the tremendous number of hours and energy to master a musical score and then to engage in the soul-searching thought to find the appropriate interpretation. But competition is also morally challenging. During her summer of Mozart, even Allegra, who is wrapped in the protective security of parents, friends, and teachers who are both caring and wise, is infected with jealousy. She suffers the foolish thoughts it inspires and experiences its ability to sour what should be a sweet experience. When Allegra discovers that an older girl named Karen is also one of the finalists in the Bloch Competition, she imagines her to be tall and majestically beautiful.

The members of the orchestra with which Karen usually plays give generous applause to Allegra when she substitutes, and treat her kindly. Even so, a chance remark she overhears between two players comparing her with Karen haunts Allegra as she prepares. Not until after the concert, when she comes face-to-face with Karen, a large ungainly girl with splotchy skin, does Allegra recognize her preconception as poisoned by her own envy.

Like Steve Landauer, Karen plays Mozart in part to escape the painful events of her life, but she is far more fully developed than Steve in accepting herself and forming relationships. Hers is a generous nature, and she is able to attend and congratulate Allegra on her stand-in performance. Karen focuses more on enjoying the music than on nursing the jealousy she could so easily have entertained for Allegra. Nineteen-year-old Karen is watching a twelve-year-old successfully perform the piece both are preparing for a competition, with her hometown orchestra. Not only is Karen generous; she is enthusiastic about other pursuits, though sometimes awkward. A wisp of Wolff's humor plays around Karen: The college girl that Allegra imagined with plucked eyebrows and a ski racing bib has mismatched clothes, and has broken her fingers while windsurfing!

When people ask how much autobiographical experience is included in *The Mozart Season*, Wolff has responded that while she began playing the violin at a relatively young age and participated in several performance groups, she never developed the expertise of Allegra at such a young age. She didn't have the same dedication as Allegra. Wolff believes that more than any inherent talent, it is that dedication to mastering a single skill or art form that makes an artist or, for that matter, a scientist or any expert, succeed. Wolff has indicated that, while one must initially be exposed to the requisite knowledge for any accomplishment, most people who seem gifted achieve mastery by hard work under the direction of a good teacher. Young people like Steve Landauer, Karen, and Allegra may seem to be especially talented, but the opportunity and the drive to devote such a large percentage of their time and energy to their art are what differentiate them. The decision to spend such a large portion of life practicing and rehearsing is complicated; as Allegra's brother indicates, it can make you a bit "crazy." In a journal article recommending books for gifted readers, Richard Olenchak summarizes this complexity as he describes Allegra's summer as a time when "she grapples with her talents and how they fit into the rest of her life" (71–73). For a healthy, sane life, much of the answer lies in balance. Besides the intense practice sessions, Allegra rides her bike, plays with her cat, and talks with her friends. Physical exercise and social contacts, Wolff indicates, are important balances to mental exploration.

Is the ability to make music a special talent, or is it inherent in all of us? In this book, Wolff implies that music is inside all of us, or perhaps inside the physical world where we can let it out. In a wonderfully playful scene, Allegra and Deirdre begin to make music by banging on the columns of an aluminum sculpted structure. The park is glorious with roses, and the splashing water adds texture to the various bonging tones. Soon one, two, and then a small crowd of passersby join in, weaving around each other as each moves to a different column to create a symphony of sound and movement. Then, almost simultaneously, they stop, the last tones dying out into "a soft hum" (74).

Deirdre poses an interesting proposition. Perhaps the purpose of humanity is to make music: "It's probably the oldest art form . . . people hopping around in caves, singing their stories, singing their prayers, banging on things, making rhythm . . . sending messages" (75). In the sense that all spoken language is tonal and rhythmic, Deirdre is making sense. In the books Wolff writes subsequent to *The Mozart Season*, Wolff focuses increasingly on capturing the characters' own voices, the authentic idiom and rhythm and music of their dialogue. In a romantic mode, Deirdre also supposes that music might already exist. "In a way, nobody was *making* music. Really, it was just a matter of letting the music out. Out of the sculpture . . . [or] whatever your instrument is" (75).

Ever the realist, Wolff has Allegra respond with a reminder that a great deal of learning and effort is necessary before most music can happen. As a young child, she had supposed that her mother and father just moved their bows to let already existing music out of their instruments. When she first tried to let music out of her own violin, she was so "shocked that there was no music coming out of it, I hid under the bed and cried and cried. There were just these screeches" (76). Wolff thus reminds her readers that before the joy of music must come the suffering. Contrary to Deirdre's romantic notion, the real world offers very little "free lunch."

Like many other writers, Wolff sometimes talks about characters popping into her imagination, their voices speaking to her as she writes. She makes it very clear, however, that the music of these characters does not simply flow out of her head onto the paper. It takes great effort and many hours to listen and then translate into comprehensible language, selecting the right words and rhythms, and shapes and tones. Like making music, writing takes long hours of effort that can be almost painful. Perhaps with enough work, all people can let their own mode of "music" emerge from whatever is their instrument of choice.

The orchestra at Trout Creek Ridge where Allegra substitutes for Karen is a group of amateurs working with their instruments. By day they are farmers, librarians, teachers, housewives, and students; not all of them can attend each practice session. But the joy that they share with anyone who attends their performances is contagious; it reaches across years of different ages, educational backgrounds, and economic situations. Allegra finds herself laughing in simultaneous pleasure with an older woman perhaps six times her age (118). The Dancing Man called Mr. Trouble is there, spreading his infectious pleasure in the melodious rhythms. All these people are connected by sharing music, by either listening or performing. While they are not all equally educated to either listen or play, each person benefits most when others participate to their fullest extent. With good effort, all can derive a modicum of beauty and communal pleasure.

The Mozart Season has received high acclaim. In 1991 it was named the School Library Journal Best Book of the Year, and in 1992 it was selected as a Janusz Korczak Honor Book, an American Library Association Notable Book, and a YALSA Best Book for Young Adults. It has been included on lists for gifted readers and lauded for its "delightful heroine" (*School Library Journal*), "as a fine achievement" (*Kirkus*) and for its "strong and intriguing characters" (*The Horn Book*). Obviously readers who are experienced musicians are especially attracted to the book, but all thoughtful readers will find much to ponder and much to enjoy; there are notes of humor as well as strains of philosophy; there is the fun of following several story lines that tease with suspense but end with satisfaction. Finally, the novel ends unexpectedly and poignantly with a grace note of romance.

References

Colburn, Nell. "The Incomparable Wolff," *School Library Journal* 48, no. 2 (February 2002).

Donat, Misha. "Mozart: Works for Violin and Orchestra," Deutsche Grammaphon. Polydor International GmbH, Hamburg, 1986.

"An Interview with Virginia Euwer Wolff." http://www.lafsd.k12. ca.us/Stanley/music/Features/Wolff_Interview/index.php. (3 Jan. 2002).

Olenchak, F. Richard. "When Gifted Readers Hunt for Books," *Voices from the Middle* 9, no. 2 (December 2001): 71–73.

Wolff, Virginia Euwer. "If I Was Doing It Proper, What Was You Laughing At?" *The Horn Book* 74, no. 3 (May 1998).

CHAPTER 4

~

Bat 6:
Dealing with Racism

Wolff decided to write *Bat 6* partly in reaction to comments about the first book of her *Make Lemonade* trilogy that features a young girl whose environment, language, and problems might seem to mark her as African-American. Many readers assumed that this book was about race. Wolff disagreed; *Bat 6* is her definition of a racist event, set in the environment she knows: the rural Northwest after World War II when racism tended to focus on the Japanese population.

The Japanese attack on the American Pacific Fleet at Pearl Harbor in Hawaii forced World War II home into the minds of the populace; it was no longer a foreign war on distant soil. More than three thousand members of the American military force were killed, all on one day, on December 7, 1941.

A panic of patriotism ensued. U.S. citizens were horrified; many were suspicious of anything Japanese, particularly the almost 300,000 people of Japanese descent who lived mainly in Hawaii and the West Coast states: California, Oregon, and Washington. Within four days, more than 1,300 Japanese living in the U.S. had been arrested, most merely on the suspicion of disloyalty.

Of course, like other immigrants, most Japanese were loyal citizens, grateful for the opportunities to earn more material wealth than was possible in Japan, and to own land, even if it was not of the best quality. But their close-knit communities, functioning somewhat apart from mainstream Americans, made them easy to identify and segregate further.

Prejudice against Japanese immigrants had long been embedded in the mainland U.S. The first Japanese arrived in California in the 1880s; they left their crowded land mainly to work on farms to save enough money to return to Japan, hoping to buy land there or start a business. But in California there was already a frontier mentality of competition against Asian immigrants from China who tended to work harder, save more money, and support each other in cooperative business ventures.

By the late 1890s, when large Japanese communities had become established in San Francisco, Los Angeles, and Seattle, and when smaller towns in the western seaboard states saw Japanese businesses and farms succeed, the ugly mood of racism began to pervade the general population, who made local laws and controlled the mainstream business community. Historically in the Western European world, when a new group settles and begins to succeed commercially, the original population becomes fearful of the new competition. Often the native culture expresses this xenophobic fear by emphasizing cultural differences, popularizing insulting labels, and spreading stories of behavior that seems potentially dangerous.

The Japanese who came to the U.S. in the decades before World War I were mainly unmarried men who, like many other immigrants (including my German grandfather), planned to work hard enough to make a good living before starting a family. In most cases, they would return to their native country to fetch a bride, and then return to settle in the U.S. Naturally, these young families retained a loyalty to their original homes and families, along with their commitment to a new life in the United States. This is particularly understandable as they were forbidden to become citizens by a narrow interpretation of the original naturalization law of 1790, which limited citizenship to "free white persons"; subsequent amendments allowed Africans and some Asians to become citizens, but Japanese immigrants were excluded. Some European Americans categorized these Japanese ties to their traditional homes and families as disloyalty to American values.

Most Japanese immigrants practiced Buddhism or other non-Christian religions, and racists called them heathens. The cultural habits of many Japanese immigrants emphasized modesty and quiet solemnity over the mainstream American frontier qualities of brashness and cheerful, easy friendliness. The popular media labeled Japanese immigrants as "inscrutable" and "sneaky" (Davis, 15).

From 1903 to 1905, about 45,000 Japanese immigrants came to the U.S., intensifying the anti-Japanese sentiment. People picketed new Japanese businesses; signs warned "Japs" not to settle in some neighborhoods. In San Francisco, in the upset after the 1906 earthquake, mobs attacked Asian businesses, and the city's schools tried to segregate Japanese schoolchildren. When the Japanese nation protested these outrages against its citizens living in the U.S., President Theodore Roosevelt negotiated the Gentlemen's Agreement of 1908 which established quotas for immigration, allowing only those who had property or families in the U.S. Further laws differentiated between the Japanese-born residents of the U.S., called Issei, who were denied citizenship, and their children who were born into citizenship, called Nisei. In 1924 all Japanese immigration was banned.

By the time of World War II, the Japanese war with China and the worsening relationship between the U.S. and Japan strengthened prejudice against both the Issei and the Nisei almost to the same point of racist hatred and repression as that experienced by African-Americans. The attack on Pearl Harbor brought to a head this long history of fear and prejudice against the Japanese. On March 21, 1942, four months after the attack, the U.S. government began a ruthless process of sequestration that would affect more than 110,000 people of Japanese descent living in the United States.

Merely on the basis of their ethnic identity, these inhabitants of U.S. soil, many of them full-fledged American citizens, were moved first to one of sixteen "assembly centers" (most in California), and then to one of ten more permanent concentration camps built especially to house them. They were given lapel tags with numbers, loaded on buses with only a limited number of their possessions, and driven to barracks that were bare of furniture and often unfinished. Most of these camps were situated on undesirable land, where the weather was unbearably hot and dusty during the summer months and bleakly cold during the winter.

Armed militia kept the interned Japanese-Americans from leaving. Concrete, wire, floodlights, and watchtowers dominated the desolate landscape. Crowded rooms and primitive toilets offended the traditionally meticulous Japanese. In his comprehensive history, *Behind Barbed Wires*, author Daniel Davis quotes former prisoner Betty Kozasa, who wept as she remembered her time there even after thirty years: "The degradation of it all, having to go to shower with 150 people, having no shower curtains" (61). Worse were toilet holes cut into a single board, barely a foot apart.

These Japanese-Americans were interned because without citizenship they were politically powerless, economically vulnerable as farmers and landholders of limited acreage, and numerically outnumbered. In contrast, the Japanese of Hawaii, where they constituted almost a third of the population, were too large a part of the economy to be managed by the government. Although many fishermen of Japanese descent lost their boats, generally they suffered much less discrimination and were never even threatened with internment.

The Japanese-Americans were interned because of the indifference of most mainstream citizens. It is too easy to get caught up in the day-to-day rhythm of managing trivial events, so that almost no one sought to help those minorities defend themselves from an overbearing governmental decision. The public was led to believe that internment was a way of protecting both U.S. citizens and Japanese-Americans from an ill-defined danger.

After the first months of shock, adjustment, and relocation to the sixteen more permanent locations, life in the internment camps became somewhat organized. Cooperative businesses were set up to take care of groceries, work, and repairs. School systems were established in each camp, most of them staffed by Nisei graduates of education schools as well as Caucasians working for the War Relocation Authority (WRA), headed by Milton Eisenhower, brother of General Dwight Eisenhower who later became president of the United States. The WRA sponsored recreational activities to ease the tensions. Adult education classes sponsored poetry, drama, and fine arts activities. Basketball and baseball teams were organized. The wonderful book for children, *Baseball Saved Us*, written by Ken Mochizuki and illustrated by Dom Lee, describes how the adults organized baseball teams to combat boredom and to keep their children actively engaged and out of the trouble too much empty time can cause. Unrest existed not only between the Caucasion government officials and the Japanese inmates, but also between the older Japanese-born Issei, who generally held to the traditional standards of humility and respectful quietness toward authority, and the younger generation, born in the United States and angered at the unjust withdrawal of their citizenship rights.

By December 18, 1944, the legal system and the government had decreed that the segregation of the Japanese was no longer necessary. Franklin Delano Roosevelt had been reelected in November and the Supreme Court had decided that keeping loyal citizens interned was no longer legal. By autumn of 1945, most of the internment camps were almost empty. However, returning to the towns and cities where they had lived before was nothing if not difficult. Many found their belongings and homes had disappeared or had been vandalized.

Many feared violence from Americans who were still prejudiced. Author Daniel Davis describes the scene that greeted Japanese returning to Hood River, Oregon. The American Legion post "had removed the names of Nisei servicemen from the town's honor roll. Three hundred Hood River residents signed a petition urging that the Japanese be welcomed back. But five hundred signed a newspaper advertisement telling the Japanese that they were not wanted" (Davis, 128). This powderkeg of conflicting feelings is the backdrop for Virginia Euwer Wolff's Bat 6.

Movie stars, celebrities, and government officials seeking public approval were now eager to give credit to the Japanese-Americans who had served so bravely in the armed forces. Few officials wanted any reprise of the anti-Japanese riots and demonstrations of earlier days. Most authority figures and most citizens in rural areas, where only a small percentage of Japanese-Americans lived, were eager for peacefulness, and the establishment of a community that could look forward to enjoying prosperity in calm, now that World War II was over. Some Japanese migrated east, away from California, Washington, and Oregon. The close-knit communities segregated from mainstream America were now loosened, and the descendants of Japanese immigrants spread throughout the continental United States. Oddly enough, the Executive Order authorizing the evacuation of Japanese-Americans from their homes was not officially revoked until more than thirty years later in 1976 by the order of President Gerald Ford.

The traditionally restrained culture of Japanese-Americans discourages them from speaking out about guilt and shame. There is a tendency to ignore issues and events that might cause embarrassment. Many

Americans growing up in the 1950s and 1960s had no idea about the hardships their fellow citizens of Japanese descent had suffered. It seemed easier for everyone to muffle the awful truth with a blanket of silence.

Born in 1937, Virginia Euwer Wolff has childhood memories, a bit vague and disjointed, of knowing that Hitler and the Japanese were the enemies in some distant evil event that existed outside their relatively peaceful community. Her mother told her how her grandparents visited a Japanese family on the night before they were forced to leave. Because this family was from Japanese aristocracy, the visit broke a social rule that dictated that they visit Wolff's grandparents first. Wolff also remembers at least one schoolmate who suddenly appeared in class in about 1945 when she was in about the third grade (allowing for the imprecision of childhood memories). She remembers a vague awareness that her schoolmate friend was Japanese, but never a sense that she had any connection with "the enemy." Wolff remembers "a kind of veil around my friend, preventing me from asking questions" (personal communication, January 2003). She surmises that neither she nor her Japanese friend knew the appropriate words to ask or how to tell about such an illogical, un-American event.

In a short story she wrote a few months before beginning to write Bat 6, Wolff reminisced about playing among the branches of a giant Douglas fir that had fallen across a road behind the school in the fall of 1944, nearly six months before peace would appear on the horizon. The boys fought the "Chaps" and the girls played house, practicing all the gestures of thrift and patriotic sacrifice they saw among the adults. But the same tree that provided so much play space for the children blocked the road and kept the letter from the government from arriving on time for Mr. J. T. McHenry to know that the worth of the ration points had changed. When the government official arrived the next week from the Office of Price Ministration, he berated the kindly, generous grocer for supposedly cheating and undermining the war effort. So distraught was J. T. McHenry that he drank down too many sleeping pills and died. The young narrator of this story remembers feeling that the fallen tree that had felt so safe had held its dangerous potential among its branches all along. "We just thought we were so safe. We weren't safe there, not ever, not even for one minute" ("A Wing and a Prayer," 78). The threat of danger that underlies the peaceful-looking surface of normal community life is the theme of Bat 6; even several years after the end of a war, the uprooted and displaced lives of children as well as adults can cause great harm in unexpected ways.

After World War II ended, most children didn't tend to speak of war or past experiences; they focused on the present trials and joys of school. In Bat 6, Wolff's characters often tune out when the adults in their midst rehearse the hardships of war. The few girls who become conscious of the internment camps express shock, but their sympathy for the Japanese-American Aki focuses more on her poverty than on her race. The girls appreciate Aki's quick intelligence, her willingness to help, and her skill with a softball. Wolff used qualities she remembers in her childhood friend to shape Aki's character: her "extreme niceness, her athleticism, her modesty" (personal communication, January 2003) and a sense of reserve in talking about her wartime experiences that seemed typical of other Japanese-American kids that Wolff remembers. More than anything, most children want to fit into a group of peers and appear as normal as they are allowed, and this included many of those who had experienced the segregation of the internment camps.

The format of Bat 6, which gives almost equal attention to twenty-one different characters, reflects the sense of community that Wolff remembers as the moral arbiter or conscience for young people. Each of the twenty-one voices describes a facet of the multi-sided complex of deeds and words that lead up to any momentous event. In this case, the event is the fiftieth annual softball game between two small rural towns within sight of Mt. Hood in Oregon.

The original community had separated into two—Bear Creek Ridge and Barlow—and a history of division and rivalry had developed. The game originated in the nineteenth century when the women, who had grown sick of the feuding, sought to counteract the bitter dissension among the men. In 1899 a group of local women decided to have a joint softball game, using a leather ball and alder branches as bats. They invited the men to watch and provided food for a picnic. This annual event continued year after year until it became a traditional game among the girls of the sixth grade, which was for many years the final grade level in the schools of both towns.

The events of Bat 6 take place in 1949, the fiftieth year of the games. Wolff celebrates the friendly spirit of this tradition in the person of

Louella, who played in the first game and who cheers for both teams because she grew up in Bear Creek Ridge and married a man from Barlow. She is considered "a hero for being so old and having her tragedies and coming to the game every year" (31). Although one of the original women peacemakers of the area, she is a victim of war; she lost her husband in the First World War and her son in the Second. Undaunted, old Louella, as the community calls her, continues to espouse the tenets of good sportsmanship and to support the friendly competition as an opportunity for healing.

Almost everyone felt the effects of World War II. People would recall making sacrifices for "the duration," a shortcut phrase for the time it would take to win the war or be invaded. For some adults it was a frightening time, especially if they had close friends or family fighting in the military. Many everyday items were rationed or in short supply. The recipe for Mrs. Rayfield's Apple Spice Cake at the end of the book suggests that the cake would not suffer with less sugar because sugar was often not available. Neither was rubber for softballs or labor to provide affordable athletic equipment. By the end of the decade, many children were sick of hearing about the war; they tuned out both the exploits of battle and the admonitions to appreciate the new luxuries of postwar days. "Men always talk about the wars, ladies always say let's forget the fighting" (83), says Lola, one of the Barlow sixth graders. Like many of the girls, she closes her ears while preparing for Bat 6, but at the end of the book she wonders why she didn't know about the hardships suffered by the Japanese-Americans, or about the terrors of Pearl Harbor. Wolff is raising a question many people ask about how much is appropriate to teach children about the horrible things that people do to each other during times of war.

In 1949 several Japanese families have become integral parts of the two communities. The Shimatsus have a little boy, Billy, who is in the first grade. The Hirokos own a strawberry farm where some of the sixth grade girls work during the summer. The Mikamis have just returned to the community after an absence of almost five years. Most people of the two communities treat them as their own, without much reference to their cultural backgrounds. They are fellow Americans, with the same order of difference that exists among all members of a community.

A class picture (cropped) shows Virginia, second from the right, second row, standing next to her friend.

Bat 6 traces the relationships among members of the two communities through the eyes of the sixth grade girls preparing for the fiftieth
softball game. The book begins with Tootie, the catcher of the Bear
Ridge team, a girl who has always preferred playing ball to playing with
dolls. The principal, concerned for her safety as the team's catcher, lends
her the mask and pads. The community is confident that the girls will
be practicing during their whole summer vacation. Even while Tootie
works at her summer job as a berry picker, she brings along her ball and
thinks about the game. When she sees Aki toss a rotten strawberry left-
handed and backwards over her shoulder, she is impressed. This girl, of
sixth grade age and apparently new to the area, has definite promise as
a player.

As a matter of fact, Aki Mikami has just returned to the Mt. Hood region after an absence of six years, more than the duration of the war. Her mother, then Keiko Ishigo, had won the award for Most Valuable Player on the softball team of 1930; her father had won a plaque for winning the spelling bee in 1924. But on May 13, 1942, the family was bundled on a train and taken to an internment camp, solely because they were of Japanese descent. Aki has only vague memories of that trying time. The train, a ticket on her lapel, and the preponderance of Japanese faces caused her to think that they had traveled away from the United States of America. After the war ended, reluctant to return to Bear Creek Ridge in rural Oregon, where the newspapers threatened that harm might come to any returning Japanese, Aki's family moved to California for several years, trying to find a place that felt safe. But in one place angry words were painted on a relative's car, and in the city the girls began to adopt the clothes, makeup, and speech of their white peers, trying to lose the parts of their identity that connected them to their Japanese heritage.

When the family finally returns to Bear Creek Ridge, they find their farm overgrown and their house ruined by irresponsible renters. Because the Mikamis had been gone for so many years, their orchard is in terrible condition. Their tractor is gone, and the quality of the fruit trees has deteriorated from years of neglect. Aki gets permission to miss days of school to help her family during harvest season; her brother misses much of high school, but he is so smart that he is able to catch up.

The community, however, welcomes them, as neighbors pitch in with gifts and supplies. Tootie invites Aki to join the team, and, despite the hardships of rebuilding a fruit farm from ruins, life seems very good.

Susannah's father had in common with Mr. Mikami that he too had won a plaque for spelling. As he is a medical doctor, he knows more about his neighbors than does the general public. Soon after the war ended in 1945, he had been called to the Shimatsus' house in the middle of the night when a white person had thrown a brick through the window and hit the baby. Perhaps because of her father, Susannah seems more aware of the extent of the suffering of others who are different, and, at the instigation of her mother, she invites Lorelei to her seventh birthday party, breaking the isolation that had lasted the length of the war. Susannah is the person who speaks for Aki when she is unable to tell her own story. Susannah is relieved to have such a good player as Aki on the team because she knows herself to be mediocre. Also, she hopes that Aki's presence will be healing in re-building the community.

During the war, Lorelei's father had been detained in a special camp because he was a conscientious objector who didn't believe in partici-pating in war. Many citizens felt that men who refused to fight in the military were almost traitorous. Catching the mood of public disap-proval, the other first grade children taunted Lorelei and left her out of their birthday parties. Now Lorelei often has to miss softball practice to help her father in the orchard because the migrant pickers refuse to work for him, even now that the war has ended. Memories are too raw. Lorelei's home is full of books, and her father often writes letters to the newspapers, sometimes to protest the prejudiced attitude against the Japanese. His enthusiasm for publicly expressing his opinions makes him seem odd to the rest of the community.

Daisy is the other outsider in first grade. A classmate has labeled her "Loose Lips" from the popular slogan "Loose lips sink ships" when she tried to share the whereabouts of her father. Daisy also feels different because she is Catholic in a town that is mostly Protestant (34). Al-though Daisy is very friendly with Lorelei, her father still does not speak to Lorelei's father, even after the end of the war, because of his refusal to fight. Daisy is embarrassed by her father's grudge, but at the same time grateful to have him back safely from the war. Secretly, Daisy hopes that on the day of the softball game her father will be so proud of her that he will forget his resentments and make peace with Lorelei's father.

Shadean's family resembles the "All-American" ideal. They live near the school and have attended every softball game since Shadean's infancy. Even when most people in the community treat Lorelei's father like a pariah, when his tractor breaks down just as he is about to set the new young pear trees he has just bought, Shadean's father volunteers to use his own new tractor to help him. Cheerful and even tempered, Shadean and her generous father are good exam-ples to the community.

Little Peggy is a tiny girl and must use a bat appropriate for her small stature. When Aki enters school, Little Peggy is often matched with her in the traditional system of lining up children in size order. Now, she considers Aki a close friend. When Aki is injured, Little Peggy feels somehow responsible: "The terrible thing is that I didn't read the invisible signs. I should have" (79), although there is no way she could have predicted or prevented Aki's accident.

Vernell's mind tends to wander. Aki helps her with her reading, but Vernell is grateful for another reason. For years she has dreaded having to play ball in public, and now that Aki has returned to the area, Vernell will not have to play. Instead, she can act as one of the team's managers. Vernell lives in an isolated area, and when she has chicken pox, she feels even more isolated than usual. Like many young girls of that generation, she has been taught to make the best of her situation; through the window she spends her time watching a heron and listens to the stories of old Louella, who lives nearby. Besides Aki, Vernell's house is the poorest, with no refrigerator.

For some families, the effect of the war has been advantageous. Ellen had moved away for about the same amount of time as Aki's family so her mother could take a job in the shipyards in Portland while her father served in the military. When Ellen's family returns to Bear Ridge Creek, they replace the outdoor privy with indoor plumbing, a new bathtub, and, for Ellen, a room of her own.

Kate, the second-base player, is ecstatic about the refrigerator her family gets at Christmas to replace their old icebox. Her father and brother are delighted that they will no longer have to haul blocks of ice from the creek, and her mother celebrates by making Jello and Kool-Aid ice cubes.

Of course there are differences among the girls on the softball team, as Kate notes: Susannah and Shadean have more material goods than the others. Ellen's family has benefited from the G.I. Bill. Lorelei's family is less well off, but Aki and Vernell have the least (72). The community of Bear Creek Ridge is better off than Barlow, where soil isn't as good and the weather has been more severe. Aki and other families have ancestors who came from Japan.

But before Shazam arrives, these differences have seemed immaterial. The girls have been members of the community in ways that seem, as one interviewer said, "so dated yet charming" (Bowlan, 11). Wolff is portraying the kind of community she remembers when she was a child, when there was "a lot of shared guilt and responsibility" (Bowlan, 11). Reminiscing with her childhood friends, Wolff remembered the small group of older men who spent their days watching over the community as they sat on the store porch. They and others communicated to parents and teachers any departure from conventional behavior. Everyone knew what all the others were doing, and that kept most people behaving well. In *Bat 6* these characters sit on the porch of McHenry's Store, reminding Tootie to keep limber for the big event coming up. The girls' mothers call each other on the telephone where a party line means anyone picking up a phone receiver can listen in. Regular meetings at church, school, and holiday celebrations are also sources of news. Sharing gossip also means that when someone is in need, the community will know and can take steps to help.

The tightness of community is palpable in *Bat 6*. Wolff wanted to portray "how everybody had a role" in raising the children and protecting the poor. Even the coaches of the rival teams are friends. Mr. Porter is officially an assistant to his wife who is the coach, and who takes pride in her service as a WAC during the war. The girls consider Mr. Porter "gorgeous" (6) despite his having lost part of his arm in service with General Patton. They appreciate his skill at explaining softball. Lorelei writes, "he was a nifty coach for he made sense about how to do things" (8). Mr. Porter is wise in other ways too. He tells his players that when they play well, they will make the Barlow team play well too. "It makes things better for everyone and that's sportsmanship" (30). Coach Rayfield and his wife are just as supportive of the Barlow team. He drives them with good advice and cheers them up when they need it, reminding them of his college-age daughter who had won Most Valuable Player of 1940. Mrs. Rayfield makes the team an apple spice cake, decorated with the names and positions of all the girls in frosting. Like Mr. Porter, Coach Rayfield is devoted to playing well, but he is a bit more competitive and yearns to win, though he would never do anything underhanded or mean.

Barlow and Bear Creek Ridge use similar tactics to solve their problems, solutions that are logical but today would induce lawsuits by citizens more interested in the purity of principles than in good common sense. When the teenage boys act up by painting a green line down the middle of Bear Creek Ridge Road to celebrate their team spirit or by moving an outhouse to the school principal's parking space at Barlow High School, the Community Council assigns them hours of community service, repairing the home of an indigent elderly woman, and cleaning up the town roads.

These boys are also barred from the privilege of attending church or going into the stores until they have completed their stint, making both of these options seem more attractive than they might to most current teenagers. The underlying message is that participation in the community is a privilege to be deserved rather than an inherent right. Most children of these two towns listen to adults seriously, with respect for their experience. The community assumes an attitude of goodwill and mutual responsibility among all its participants. Little of the girls' gossip about each other is in any way mean-spirited. From memories of her own childhood, Wolff portrays "that small reach toward nobility kids incorporated into their lives" (Bowlan, 11). How could any violent act of racism take place among such good intentions and aspirations?

Shazam, who plays outfield for Barlow, is damaged goods. Born outside of the community, she has been reared with a misguided hatred for the Japanese soldiers who she believes have ruined her life by killing her father. New to school at the beginning of the sixth grade year, Shazam arrives wearing an awkwardly home-made dress and boys' shoes that the other girls recognize as from a rummage sale. Her given name is Shirley but she demands to be called Shazam, like the magic word that comic book hero Captain Marvel speaks to produce his bolt of lightning. Brita Marie notes that Shazam has "steel eyes" (14) and strong arms. Both left- and right-handed, a strong hitter and a good runner, Shazam is obviously a welcome addition to the Barlow team. She turns out to be such a good player that the sixth grade boys who volunteer to practice with the girls begin to feel threatened by her skill. Her expertise with a softball goes a long way in muffling the effect of her social ineptitude and strange remarks in reference to the Japanese. Softball is obviously a priority to several of the girls.

Brita Marie is kind. Although her parents own the Barlow General Store, she is anything but spoiled. On the first day of school Brita Marie feels protective of Shazam, mentally hurting for her odd clothes and wishing she did not have to suffer for being so terribly different. The sixth grade teacher, Mrs. Winters, assigns her as Shazam's mentor. Shazam is so lacking in both mental and social skills that the job is overwhelming.

Obviously, Shazam has not attended much school in previous years, because she has few math or reading skills. Neither has she learned social skills. The girls try to teach her how to act in church and encourage her not to stare at physical deformities, but their lessons are slow to take. When Audrey and Wink try to teach her the multiplication tables, she only succeeds halfway. She tends to blame her tutors when the work becomes difficult for her.

Audrey, the Barlow team's catcher, strengthens her arms by stacking firewood with Darlene. Her uncle Beau works at the gas station where he has painted a large sign with the scores of all forty-nine games on it, Barlow's in red and those of Bear Creek Ridge in green. Good at arithmetic, she is assigned to teach Shazam the times table.

Wink, the first baseman for Barlow, stands at five feet and ten inches, noticeably taller than the others. She is a good hitter. At her birthday party, she shows the girls the professional baseball jersey her mother had made with the number of her idol, Hank Greenberg of the Detroit Tigers. She is fascinated by his Jewish identity that seems slightly exotic to Wink who has grown up in a predominantly Protestant town (86).

Ila Mae is the pitcher of the Barlow Bat 6 team. She thinks about pitching constantly and, just as often as she can, practices with her brother A.J., who is glad to help her. Like Allegra of *The Mozart Season*, who is devoted to her music, and Nick of *Probably Still Nick Swansen*, who counts on his study of amphibians to make his day worthwhile, Ila Mae is in love with softball. She has long dreamed of earning the Most Valuable Player award. So avid is she to succeed that she soaks her hands in pickle brine to toughen them up.

Darlene has the "fastest overhand in Barlow history" (15) and can throw a long ball better than most others. Her father, the snowplow driver, tells her all about the animals he sees early in the morning. Her mother cleans house for Susannah's family and the two young girls play together until she finishes. Darlene feels that she has the least material wealth on the team, but the coach has convinced her that she is special because of her overhand and needs to improve her grades to guarantee a spot on the team. She does study, earning the respect of her teacher as well as the approval of her coach.

Lola and Lila are twins, and they speak simultaneously until toward the end of the book. In many sets of twins, one dominates in social interactions while the other gets subsumed in the role of the other twin. In this town the twins are treated like a single entity. When Shazam arrives, the twins lose a chance for a spot on the team and are assigned as managers and general subs. While the others cheer them on for their efforts, Lola seems to harbor some bitterness, especially when Shazam's actions prevent the game from being fully played.

As soon as Coach Rayfield sees Shazam perform, he asks her to play outfielder. When he jokingly suggests to Manny that she must have prayed for a good outfielder, the girls get the impression that Shazam was somehow fated to help the Barlow team win.

Manny, or Manzanita, is considered a bit different since she "got the spirit" (49) at a tent revival. Though not particularly fanatical about her religion, she testifies to visions and quotes the voice of God in ways that make the others wonder about the soundness of her judgment, particularly on the baseball field. Manzanita believes that God wants her to do her best, and sees no conflict between what her teachers and coach want her to do and what is God's will. She listens carefully to the voices that reveal His will to her, and she tries to obey as responsibly as she can. Hers is a sincerely felt faith.

Shazam is a mystery to the other girls; they know that she lives with her grandmother by the gravel pit and that their mothers refer to her as "Floy's girl, poor little thing" (22). Eventually they hear the rumor that her mother conceived her out of wedlock. Later the girls learn that Floy had been rather wild. Shazam's father had a criminal record and had run away from his responsibilities by joining the Navy; he was killed at Pearl Harbor.

Alva, Barlow's shortstop, gets down on her knees in shock when she hears that Shazam's mother had quit school and gotten pregnant with Buzz, who had stolen a car. "Poor Shazam. Her mother a sinner and her crook father dead. No wonder she got so tangled in her face" (65). Buzz had refused to marry Floy, Shazam's mother, and had abandoned her as well as his job when he joined the Navy. Alva wonders if she should keep this secret to protect Shazam from feeling ashamed, or if she should tell it so others will be as sympathetic. In her prayer to God, she poses all her questions as well as her problems. While she is grateful that God has provided an opportunity for her to earn money for a new glove, she has further requests. Could God grant her father a job so her mother can have her teeth fixed? Alva suffers embarrassment for her mother's bad teeth. Her prayer is a mélange of gossip, shock, innocent generosity, and self-serving requests. Alva's audience with the Lord is wryly amusing as she naively juxtaposes genuine shock at the real tragic consequences of war and the more superficial concern about her mother's appearance. Her faith seems more an expression of adolescent melodrama than a sincere concern for the welfare of her fellow humans, particularly in relation to Shazam.

In her bedroom, Shazam displays a puka-shell necklace that her father gave her on her third birthday, while they were living in Hawaii; it was the last time she remembers seeing him. Evidently Shazam has learned her hatred for the Japanese from her mother: "My mom she hit me I forgot the gas mask I said I forgot she said don't dare forget them Japs bomb us again you die without no gas mask I won't have nobody" (111). As in *The Mozart Season* when Allegra's parents resort to anger to mask their fear that their daughter might come to harm, Floy displaces her fear by angrily abusing her child. Most readers have been conditioned to disapprove of Floy for her irresponsibility, but she is the kind of war victim that passes her anger and incompetence on to her child. Shazam cannot think straight about anything without visions of fire, bombs, and the noise of her mother's crying. Floy lacks the resilience to handle tragedy; she has neither the skills nor the moral strength to rear a healthy child by herself, and she lives outside of a community.

Shazam's athletic perseverance is partly motivated by her anxiety, which veers into paranoia: "You never know one of them might sneak up behind your back like they done my dad. I saw them" (84). Shazam has recurrent dreams of a fire from which nobody can escape. These dreams interrupt her concentration on the numbers she is trying to learn. They awaken her at night, and she looks at a string of puka shells from her father, who was killed at Pearl Harbor.

It is Ila Mae who first overhears Shazam use the word "Jap." They are walking to school when six-year-old Billy Shimatsu runs by, also on the way to school. "Hey, there's a Jap. Right in this school," comments Shazam. When Ila protests, Shazam asks, "Don't you remember Pearl Harbor?" (26). Ila Mae explains to her that the word "Jap" is considered derogatory and is not allowed in school. When Shazam protests, Ila Mae distracts her by talking about softball and starting a game of catch. I should of caught on . . . I promised God I would keep it a secret. I just didn't catch on. Then" (26).

Another member of the team also keeps her awful knowledge secret. Beautiful Hair Hallie is an attractive girl with the confidence to be generous to others. Her family has material comforts, partly because of the military benefits her father has earned. Her athletic prowess and the tresses that have instigated the nickname she would rather not acknowledge have made her a popular figure in the community. Hallie owns an excellent softball glove and a talent to match for fielding grounders and stealing bases. Shazam is attracted to her and asks to practice with her. When Hallie explains that her father became deaf in one ear as a result of the war, she is shocked to hear Shazam blame the "Japs." She is even more shocked when Shazam blurts out that her father had been killed by the "Japs'" bombing of Pearl Harbor. "The whole Navy tried to save him, them Japs made my mom a widow" (58). Hallie recognizes that Shazam is not rational, that her use of the derogatory term is unforgiving, but she also feels sorry for the fatherless girl who lives with her grandmother.

Though Hallie tells her friends about the death of Shazam's father, she decides not to tell them about Shazam's prejudicial anger. "I was grown up enough to keep that bad secret. And I had told Shazam she couldn't say it anymore. I had done my part" (62). Shazam is an unpredictable and uncomfortable person to be around. Hallie is glad she has made Shazam so happy by inviting her over to practice, but she feels more sympathy for the Utsumi family who live on her family's farm.

This book seems like a movie script. The story unfolds in stages, first the voices of girls from the Bear Creek Ridge team, then a chapter of memories from a few Barlow players. The shape is similar to the budding of a rose, where a petal opens on one side, and then is matched by another on the other side. Finally the whole flower is open and the genesis of the flower is visible; the pistil and the stamen finally evolve into flower petals, just as Shazam's assault on Aki is both the genesis and the result of this tale. Fortunately, this act of violence is not the end of the story.

After the assault, the community is in an uproar. The fiftieth game is never finished. Fights break out. The crowd erupts into a hubbub. Some are angry, and some are so weighed down by guilt that they withdraw. Then the community begins to heal again. Wolff does not even pretend to fully solve the problem of the broken children in our midst who, like Shazam, have learned more about fear and blame than love and community. However, she points at the beginning of a process of healing. Daisy's father disregards his grudge against Lorelei's father for not fighting in the war, and Lorelei's father accepts his social overture gracefully; they sit together in public. After the shock wears off, the Community Council asks the girls from each team to report what they saw and what they know.

It isn't the girls' formal responses that make up the chapters of the book, but what this request generates in their minds. Like the language of Nick in *Probably Still Nick Swansen*, the dialect of these girls is often ungrammatical and uneven in tone. Often their narratives reveal their burgeoning realization that other people have their own secrets and complications.

Like William Faulkner and all the writers who have imitated his style, Wolff is revealing her characters through their voices with all their particular quirks of logic and association. Her writing is not stream of consciousness, because the girls are addressing an audience; some are thinking out what they want to say to the committee; others are praying to their God. They seem to be explaining the incident to themselves by articulating their memories. Without a character list or a visual reference, the memories or commentaries of twenty-one voices are hard to follow on a first reading. Although the element of surprise and suspense is missing, rereading the novel with a consciousness of the plot brings the reward of being able to focus on the personal development of many characters. In a second reading, the subtle interrelationships among the girls become more obvious, as the details unfold about their relative social and economic status, their religion and their relationship to their parents. *Bat 6* has the vivid characters and engaging plot that could inspire an effective film; the scriptlike style of unfolding the story would facilitate this project in the hands of a director sensitive to the historical time period and the subtle nuances of the characters' words.

Wolff realizes that the large number of separate voices, twenty-one altogether, is difficult for some readers to comprehend, but she wanted to demonstrate a democratic sensibility; she wanted to include a wide variety of voices. Just as a recently popularized slogan asserts that it takes a village to raise a child, Wolff "wanted a village to tell a story" (Sutton, 283). The terrible assault that shatters this annual celebration of peace is committed by a single individual. But the whole community takes responsibility and tries to heal the breach. Aki's family receives visits, flowers, and more practical gifts from neighbors in Bear Creek Ridge as well as from strangers from Barlow. The Community Council assigns the task of helping build a deer fence for the Mikamis to Shazam, under the direction of Aki's older brother, Shig. Shazam, however, seems almost unconscious of what she has done, and the community remains conflicted about how to treat her. One of the young players, however, decides to take direct action.

Manzanita, also called Manny, credits God with convincing her to befriend Shazam. Knowing that she will raise the ire and scorn of her friends, she is determined to obey, even when her first efforts seem fruitless. She gets courage from Jesus whom she hears in her own language: "Manzanita, Child of God, Christian goodness ain't easy, you try again" (209) and "Manny, you have the gumption of the Lord, now use it" (210). She borrows a bike and takes Shazam to Aki's house, threatening the reluctant girl with the magical power of Jesus, while silently hoping that God will forgive her for the lies she knows she is telling.

Manny wants to nudge Shazam into apologizing to Aki, but Shazam does not seem to recognize that she has been responsible for Aki's injury. Warnings and reminders of Pearl Harbor, urged on her by her mother with the strength of repeated blows, have numbed her mind against new perceptions of anything related to the Japanese. She has trouble tracking new ideas. Only when Aki tells her the truth about how badly she is hurt does Shazam begin to acknowledge her own guilt. The tension is exquisite in the scene near the end of the book where Aki struggles to break through her habit of polite self-denial, taught to her both by her cultural traditions and her experience in the United States of the 1940s. Finally Aki is honest and Shazam understands. The polite conventions of the community and the sense of mutual responsibility must be taught; Shazam has not been civilized. Neglected by her mother who is evidently a wounded soul herself, Shazam needs the kind of parental direction that Manny, in her earnest faith, is prompted to provide.

As in *The Mozart Season*, Wolff ends the book with a coda of sweet promise. While Shazam is working with Shig on the fence, her fear of contact with the Japanese is evidently melting. When the older boy touches her arm so she will notice a deer, she responds with no fear. Instead, she is charmed by the sight. But Wolff knows that prejudice is not that easy to heal and refuses to sentimentalize her story with a facile, happy ending. The next page is Alva's report which indicates that her Christianity is not as generous as Manny's. Alva wonders why Shazam doesn't just leave the community so their troubles will be over. "How much Christian goodness do we have to learn?" (229). Wolff's book ends with this honest indication that breaking the circle of fear, war, and the resulting resentments is a task that takes continual vigilance, caring, and authentic communication.

Wolff's softball players are very conscious of their relationship with God, though their words reflect different concepts of their personal relationships with a deity. Peggy expects God to be rational in response to her prayers; she isn't surprised that Aki doesn't die. "God wouldn't take away my best friend; I knew that wouldn't be a reasonable thing for God to do" (184). Manny's Christianity is a less logical, more visceral experience; she hears God's voice and sees Jesus. During times of high excitement, Manny's passion bursts forth as a chant of words that make more sound than sense. Alva's relationship with God seems more self-centered than thoughtful. Although Wolff portrays Manny's faith as somewhat naïve, she honors the results of her actions. Wolff further explores various aspects of faith and religion in her next book, *True Believer*.

Though *Bat 6* has not received as high a number of accolades as Wolff's previous two books, it has earned several prestigious awards. It was one of the New York Public Library's 100 Best Books of the Year in 1998, and selected as a School Library Journal Best Book of the Year for the same year. Wolff was particularly pleased at its receiving the Jane Addams Peace Award in 1999 as an effort to "promote peace and equality" (Gallo, 4). The book was also named an American Library Association Notable Book in 1990 and placed on the Volunteer State Young Adult Book Award Master List for 2001–2002.

Critic Don Gallo calls it a "gutsy book to have written" (Gallo, 3) for its exploration of prejudice from a perspective unique among writers of young adult literature. Wolff admits that writing it was a difficult experience. However, the option of forever wondering how the characters' stories would resolve would have been an equally difficult choice. Wolff credits her literary agent, Marilyn Marlow, with encouraging her to complete the project, even when she herself felt discouraged.

Undoubtedly, as interest in the effect of the Japanese internment rises as a comparison to the present treatment of Arab Americans, more teachers and activists will take notice of this perceptive analysis of racial bigotry that pulls at the heart while it pokes holes in the boundaries of the mind.

References

Armor, John, and Peter Wright. *Manzanar*. Photographs by Ansel Adams. Commentary by John Hersey. Times Books, 1988.

Bowlan, Cheryl. "Interview with Eugene Euwer Wolff," *Contemporary Authors Online*. The Gale Group, 2001. http://www.galenet.com (3 Jan. 2002).

Davis, Daniel. *Behind Barbed Wire: The Imprisonment of Japanese Americans During World War II*. E. P. Dutton, 1982.

Gallo, Don. "Virginia Euwer Wolff." Interview. Authors4Teens.com. http://www.authors4teens.com/A4T?source=interview&authorid=wolff (16 Jan. 2001)

Mochizuki, Ken. *Baseball Saved Us*. Illustrated by Dom Lee. Scholastic, 1993.

Wolff, Virginia Euwer. "A Wing and a Prayer." *Kid's Stuff: Left Bank Collection Number 6*, edited by Linny Stovall. Hillsboro, Ore.: Blue Heron, 1994.

CHAPTER 5

~

Make Lemonade:
Learning Compassion

Virginia Euwer Wolff has credited Salinger's "For Esmé—With Love and Squalor" as one of the few stories that made her know that she would someday be a writer. The recognition of a poignantly painful undercurrent to even the most pleasant moments of modern life seems to resonate with Wolff. Her quest to let her characters speak directly to the interior life of intelligent readers connects her to Salinger's early important work.

The narrator of Salinger's "For Esmé—With Love and Squalor" describes the rainy day in April 1944 when he enjoyed a conversation over tea with the thirteen-year-old British Esmé and her younger brother Charles, whose parents had both been killed. Esmé is a born leader, with a self-possession that comes from honest inquiry into her circumstances and a forthright acceptance of the hard facts she finds. She asks for no sympathy; rather, she is exceedingly generous and thoughtful as she entertains the American soldier, sharing her story and asking him intelligent and thoughtful questions. Using adult vocabulary, obviously garnered from reading the dictionary, she inserts herself into the adult world as an equal participant, confident that her help is of worth equal to whatever she may accept. What Esmé requests from this soldier who writes stories is that he write one for her that isn't "childish and silly" (*Nine Stories*, 100). "Make it extremely squalid and moving" (103), she reminds him as they part. Her proclaimed interest in "squalor" indicates her preference not only for honest realism but also for the parts of life that reach down into our hearts, the experiences of striving from the core of our being toward others through boundaries that seem impossible. To reach from the squalid part of ourselves, the blood and bone and sinew of our consciousness where emotions are sticky and raw and frightening, and to reach toward another with an honesty that is also frighteningly clear, seem to be Salinger's concept of love.

Esmé shows that kind of love when she sends the soldier-narrator a letter that contains her father's watch "for the duration of the conflict" as a "lucky talisman" (113). Both reach the narrator in the hospital and help pull him back from post-traumatic depression to a place where he can write a story for her with all the serious tenderness of "love and squalor." The stories of LaVaughn and Jolly in *Make Lemonade* and its sequel are, I think, Wolff's messages "with love and squalor" to the young people she has met or learned about who strive to climb impossible walls and do so with the kind of persistence and resilience that should astound us all.

Wolff's fascination with young characters who survive difficult situations inspired the story of Jolly. The narrator is LaVaughn, who speaks about her motivation to seek work as a babysitter for Jolly and to become involved in her life. LaVaughn uses the advice from her mother and the lessons from her classes in school to guide her in helping Jolly become a successful mother.

LaVaughn's home is public housing in a neighborhood where gangs, drug dealing, and pimping abound, to the extent that a Watchdog Committee takes turns guarding the entrances to their building and all the girls are required to take self-defense classes. LaVaughn's father was murdered by a stray shot as he played basketball nearby. Nobody in the sixty-four apartments of the building has ever been to college; LaVaughn plans to be the first. Her mother has taught her to be clean and organized, and insists that she finish all her homework and other tasks. Her life is hard, but not squalid.

Squalor surrounds and threatens to bury Jolly. Even the sign she has left on the bulletin board, where LaVaughn first sees the advertisement for a babysitter, is smudged and wrinkled. Her apartment reeks with unpleasant odors, the garbage cans are open, and the floor is sticky. She meets LaVaughn "jouncing a gooey baby in her arms and something gurgles out of [her] nose" (6). Even the words Wolff uses to describe Jolly's apartment sound gross. At Jolly's house, "the plates are pasted together with noodles and these rooms smell like last week's garbage" (23). The squalor is so overwhelming to LaVaughn that she makes a C-minus on her social studies test, and she doesn't even know yet what real squalor is.

Real squalor is when things don't grow, like the lemon seeds LaVaughn plants for Jolly's two-year-old son, Jeremy. Or when Jolly comes home with "her whole face scraped like it had a grater taken to it, like it was cheese" (33) and she has nobody to take care of her. Or when her boss puts his hand under her clothes and she gets fired from the job that is paying for the rent and the heat and the toilet paper for herself and her two children, both under the age of three. Real squalor is when there is nobody to tell you things: no folks, no teachers, no friends, and no girlfriends, and it seems impossible to "take hold." Jolly has been homeless; she has lived in a box with other children who deal in drugs, sex, and whatever gets them through the day. Even with a minimum-wage job and no medical benefits or insurance, Jolly has raised herself from where she has been.

Walter Dean Myers, in his acceptance speech for the 2000 Michael Printz award, made note of the small number of novels dealing with the lives of inner-city adolescents published and reviewed in mainstream review journals. Hughes-Hassell and Gould analyze fourteen YA novels that focus on the lives of urban minorities selected from the only twenty such novels published in the decade of the 1990s (Hughes-Hassell and Guild, 35). These novels share several characteristics that make them relevant to urban teens. *Make Lemonade* is cited as an example of literature that avoids stereotyping the inner-city poor by portraying different levels of poverty and various ways of reacting to it. While this book illustrates the ugliness of poverty and fear, it also depicts a community that offers opportunities for support to its members despite the serious dangers present.

LaVaughn and her mother live in a subsidized apartment. There is little money to spare, and they achieve a small measure of security only by organizing the tenants to be constantly vigilant. In comparison with Jolly's apartment, however, their home is a haven of comfort and security. LaVaughn is struggling in school to maintain her grades so she might eventually apply to college, but she can see a clear light at the end of the tunnel of her life. Even so, only a thin line divides her life from Jolly's. She can easily imagine that, with the loss of her mother, or an unwanted pregnancy, or any of a number of other accidents, she herself could end up in a similar situation. So it is especially generous of LaVaughn to spend time and energy on Jolly and her two children. She is taking the risk that her own ambitions will slip into the background, letting her fall into the black hole of Jolly's life, surrounded by squalor.

From the beginning, it is obvious that LaVaughn is kind. When she and her friends look for jobs at school, LaVaughn responds to the messiest note on the bulletin board because it has obviously attracted no previous attention. When she arrives at Jolly's apartment, she is repelled by the filth and the impossible mess. The children ooze with disgusting dampness, and dirt is rubbed into every corner, but when she hears the desperation in Jolly's voice and feels two-year-old Jeremy's hand in hers, she accepts the babysitting job. *Make Lemonade* is the story of LaVaughn's love for Jolly and her children, and the effect of that love.

"Love" is a word easily prostituted, but Wolff shows us the authentic, compassionate love that is gratingly difficult to live. This rare kind of love, the kind Esmé demands in Salinger's story and the kind that she gives, can be the medium for growth that seems miraculous, like the growth of lemon seeds that are picked out of the garbage, stuck in common dirt, and only in rare instances, after long days of light and careful watering, sometimes sprout.

LaVaughn's relationship to Jolly begins because of her compassion for someone who is in need. She plans her campaign to gain her mother's permission to babysit by listing seven rationales. The fourth and fifth reasons reveal her sympathetic nature: "that sideways look of Jolly's eyes / like a car will come out of nowhere & run her down" (15) and "that sound in Jolly's voice, / that 'I can't' she says over and over again" (15). Jeremy's hand in hers, reason number seven, is what clinches her nurturing sense, and it is what finally convinces her mother that she is capable.

LaVaughn describes her mother as "a big Mom," a mom who goes to work earlier than LaVaughn goes to school, cooks dinner, and spends hours and hours to keep the building safe. Her mother insists on conversations with her daughter. LaVaughn knows that her mother notices everything she does, that she has "an attention span that goes on for years" (12). When LaVaughn, then in the fifth grade, mentions that she would like to attend college, her mother warns her that it will take money, hard work, persistence, and she doesn't know what else, but she also assures her that they can make it happen. If LaVaughn goes to college, it will make her prouder than any other accomplishment. It is especially LaVaughn's mother, her constant attentions and the urgency of her discipline, that makes LaVaughn's life different from Jolly's. LaVaughn's mother imposes order on their world. She makes rules for keeping that structure firm, insisting on help around the house, homework done before play, and respect from her daughter. She works cooperatively with other tenants to put mirrors in the elevators, to set up a self-defense class for girls once they reach the age of ten, and to establish a Watchdog Committee that guards the door against strangers. Having lost her husband, she is fervent about keeping her daughter tethered to anything that might keep her safe, and focused on achieving a better future. At this point in their lives, that is the established structure of school. LaVaughn's mother checks on her homework religiously and preaches messages urging hard work and obedience. Jolly's life, barely on the margin of the established social institutions, could threaten LaVaughn's success in school, and her mother grants her permission to babysit only "on condition. On condition that you keep those grades up" (19). LaVaughn's mother loves her daughter with a fierce protectiveness that is partly for her own sense of pride, but is all-enveloping. She has little maternal energy to spare for anyone but her daughter.

Soon LaVaughn recognizes the risk she has taken on by getting involved with Jolly and her children. When her school friends, Myrtle and Annie, notice how LaVaughn finishes her homework instead of eating lunch, they predict that her grades will suffer. LaVaughn's test grades do slip, and, when Jolly doesn't come home for two days, she also misses a day of school. Jolly finally does come home with her face bleeding, and LaVaughn feels that she has to call her mother to come and help. Now that her mother knows how young and defenseless Jolly is, she is proud of her daughter's compassion but even more afraid that LaVaughn's dream of college will be threatened. She suggests that LaVaughn find another job, but by now it's too late. "That Jolly she's got hold of you" (42), she says to her daughter, and it's true. LaVaughn has persisted and finally succeeded in toilet training Jeremy; she has taught him how to make his bed "out of self-respect," and forgiven him when he cut off his sister's curls. She and Jolly have even had the time to share the kind of laughter that makes the world seem safe for a while. LaVaughn worries about the children's future. She has invested important parts of herself in their lives.

Then Jolly gets fired from her job. It's a clear case of sexual harassment, but with no money for a lawyer and a desperate need for work, she has no power to accuse him. She needs LaVaughn to sit for the children so she can look for work, but she can't pay her. LaVaughn is in a quandary. How much should she give up of her own dreams to save Jolly and the children from certain homelessness and despair? What does compassion demand of her? What is the boundary between selfishness and self-preservation?

If LaVaughn isn't earning money, she isn't reaching toward her goal of college. When Jolly asks to borrow the money from her college fund, money that will never be returned, LaVaughn thinks for a minute and refuses. However, she does continue to sit for Jolly's children, and she begins to ask for help. Her mother suggests welfare, but Jolly is afraid of losing her children. A teacher suggests a special program for single mothers, but Jolly balks; she has never been successful in school, and her lack of spelling skills is visible evidence. LaVaughn is discovering other holes in Jolly's development too; when Jolly visits the school, she hides her fear with a posture that looks insolent. When she talks to authorities who could help her, she answers with as few words as possible. She can't decide what words to use on the application form. So LaVaughn slowly and painstakingly leads her through the process of reaching toward help and enlisting her in a program that will teach her the skills to improve her situation. Meanwhile, LaVaughn's mother is huffing her disapproval in the background, and LaVaughn's friends Myrtle and Annie accuse Jolly of being a bad influence.

Now that Jolly seems to be on the way to helping herself, LaVaughn ponders the nature of helping others. "You have to find the good thing / that ain't the wrong good thing, / like for somebody going to abuse you, / or like you expect some big banquet of thanks for it / which you ain't going to get" (120). LaVaughn is proud of what she has accomplished for Jolly and her children. Her grades are improving, and one of her teachers notices that she is responding more quickly with less exhaustion. Everything seems to be back to normal, and Jolly and her children seem safe. Now that Jolly is attending school, LaVaughn feels that she has graduated from something, also "like somebody took a chunk out somewhere / and didn't put it back" (117). She has paid a price; real charity means that time, energy, and thought that cannot be replaced have been expended.

Many novels would end here, a simple happy ending full of hopeful indications for major breakthroughs. But Wolff is too knowledgeable about children of poverty, and too honest to write simplistically. Just as Jolly is making good grades and gaining confidence, she misses three days of school because Jeremy gets the chicken pox, and she begins to fall behind in her homework. The school will pay LaVaughn to babysit again for Jolly's children for an hour, but her delight at returning to the children is soured by spikes of resentment and judgment. Jolly doesn't seem to concentrate; she doesn't seem to finish everything she starts, and she is careless. LaVaughn loses patience and blames Jolly for not using birth control.

She has hit Jolly too hard; Jolly returns in kind, and lets LaVaughn know what it's really like to be without defenses. Birth control has no relevance when someone bigger and stronger is in charge: "Sometimes you don't have time, / . . . They get in a hurry, / they forget you're even around" (131), hisses Jolly. Then she lets loose with a tirade of accusations: Ms. LaVaughn thinks she is Ms. Perfect; she has preempted parts of Jolly's children, and she makes Jolly feel inept and left out. The breath is sucked out of both of them as they drag each other through their most squalid feelings. And then, at the last second before she leaves the apartment perhaps forever, LaVaughn's compassionate caring nature takes over. Sinking to her knees, she grasps Jolly's knees, and the two dissolve their anger into tears. Then Jolly asks LaVaughn for something that will help them start all over again; she asks LaVaughn to retell the story of her mother and their friends when they made themselves look ridiculous by putting Vaseline on their faces just before a dusty auto race. It is a silly story, but it transforms their tears and regrets into cleansing laughter.

What they begin again is the same old relationship, both struggling to get through school, both helping the children struggle into childhood. Jeremy gets glasses; Jilly walks for the first time. The house stays dirty, and the homework is hard, but they persist. Then, when Jilly swallows a plastic toy, Jolly saves her life using the CPR skills she has learned in school and by not giving up, even after LaVaughn is sure that the infant is dead. The weeks pass by, but Jolly seems to have a new hold on her life. That hold, however, seems tenuous, and the book ends on an ambivalent note.

Novels for young adults rarely have pessimistic endings, where the characters still lack a stable connection to the mainstream and seem to be running out of options. Realistic, optimistic endings give necessary hope to adolescents who lack the long-term experience to see that pain and loss can be softened over time, making even the most severe tragedies bearable. In a journal article about the various endings of literature for young people, Nobles quotes the definition by YAL experts Kenneth Donelson and Aileen Nilsen of an optimistic ending in which characters make worthy accomplishments: "The most powerful optimistic ending has the protagonist actually take a next step based on . . . self-revelation" (Nobles, 48). In *Make Lemonade* Jolly returns to school and finally commits herself to improving her life through education. After she saves her baby from dying, she seems to gain a new confidence; she is taking hold. Her classes continue, and she has a babysitting pool, so she rarely calls LaVaughn. LaVaughn's classes are going well and she has new after-school jobs, but she feels a bit wistful. "It's completely different now. / I been broken off, / like part of her bad past. / I was the one that knew the saddest parts of Jolly, I guess" (198).

In her article, Nobles delineates three types of optimistic endings in YA novels. The first offers instant satisfaction to many young readers. The big problems of the book are solved, in a fairy tale ending. Such easy wish-fulfillment endings appear at the end of most popular movies and TV shows. Jolly is hoping for this kind of solution to her problems when she writes a letter to a philanthropic billionaire who rewards people he deems "deserving" (148). She expends more energy than usual, even rewriting her letter several times without complaint. But the billionaire sends her only five dollars to buy a treat for her children. This is not a book where a heroic knight or a Prince Charming will solve a problem just by magic.

A second more moderate type of happy ending shows the character learning how to live wisely and well, experiencing positive consequences of his or her worthy actions. This kind of ending often exemplifies what the author considers the proper way to conduct a life. Wolff tries not to be explicitly didactic although good advice often comes through her characters' voices.

The third type of optimistic ending is the most restrained and realistic. It emphasizes the continuing enormous challenges confronting the characters and it offers no diverting wish-fulfillment attainments. Above all, it evolves naturally out of all the circumstances and character developments that come before. The most optimistic endings to Wolff's novels are hopeful in the sense that a character gains insight that will eventually lead to positive steps toward a kinder life. This is the best that Wolff hopes from real people in real circumstances, and she writes only stories that are as realistic as she honestly can make them.

Wolff is a writer who conceives of characters in a particular situation and then listens to their voices rather than giving them messages to deliver. From her own experiences, both lived and vicarious, she imagines the logical possibilities of her characters' lives, given the parameters of their personalities and historical situations. As a child, Wolff had the rug suddenly pulled out from beneath the extraordinarily happy home life she remembers before she was five; she did not develop into a person who expects an easy solution to life's problems. Her experiences learning to play complex classical music on the violin teach her the continual perseverance and hard work necessary to succeed; she does not expect good-quality results to come without such diligent effort and without a simultaneous process of inner questioning and critical growth.

The narrator of Make Lemonade is conscious that "reality" is partly shaped from within, that memory can be a slippery thing, shaping an experience in a person's mind by how many details are included and how they are interpreted. The book begins with LaVaughn's assurance: "I am telling you this just the way it went" (3). But then, qualifying her first statement, she admits that she is including all the details she remembers, and perhaps she has not understood everything about what did happen. Experiencing second thoughts about how accurate this version of her story is, the narrator LaVaughn becomes more tentative about her own memories, comparing them with a bird, eating on a sidewalk in front of you one minute, gone the next.

The slippery nature of truth is a frame for the story. Section 66, the last in the book, refers back to this tentative beginning—"Sometimes the most real thing I remember isn't . . ."—followed by a list of four incidents. "Sometimes" is repeated in the next sentence with another list of happier incidents not remembered. The next stanza begins with a third "Sometimes," but rewards the reader with the memory that sticks, the joyous picture of Jeremy forgetting "the fear and all the hardness" (200). Even just for a moment "he is a cheerful child / a boy in the air, ready for his dinner" as he laughs down at LaVaughn's Big Mom, the strongest source of certitude and truth in the novel, "looking up there to him, her mouth wide open and full of praise" (200). If LaVaughn's mother, so cautious with her approval and so suspicious of any good that LaVaughn can find in Jolly and her family—if SHE can open her mouth with praise, it must be trustworthy. Even more than the lemon sprig beginning to sprout from the seed (a sprout we all know might turn sickly, or wilt or die), this strong woman's approval is an image of hope. Although she herself isn't absolutely confident in her judgment, LaVaughn's strongest memory is one of hope, and, after all, this is her story.

Make Lemonade began as a creative writing exercise, where Wolff decided to write in a persona other than her own. She decided to write as a babysitter, and "out came the first 5 lines of section 7" (Author-Chats, 4). The title came from a quote of the well-known maxim that she first noticed in the *New York Times*. So struck was she by the concept that she cut it out to save: "If you get lemons [in life], make lemonade." But *Make Lemonade* was also inspired by Wolff's empathy for people who are left out of the system and must struggle to manage a decent life. She had watched a television series about the generations of poor Americans who cannot seem to escape the cycle of poverty and danger. While feeling sorrow and discouragement at the enormity of the problems faced by the poor and those who try to escape, she was also impressed by the "tough, angry, loving women who take justice and safety into their own hands in inner-city projects"; Wolff felt that she could "write poor talk because [she had] been poor in spirit" (Zvirin, 1251). She had lived in city apartments with small children and felt deep despair. And so she was able to write about LaVaughn and Jolly.

Of course, Wolff had more courage and resources inside herself than she knew. While attending a workshop to enable her to end her lifetime habit of smoking, she learned that she could accomplish most of what she wanted to do; her life was in her hands, and just needed to be lived. So she was able to write LaVaughn's mother too, a woman with such courage and determination that it swelled her into a person who seemed big to her daughter and, indeed, to the other people around her. Faced with the sudden death of her husband and the responsibility of rearing a child alone, she took hold of her life and managed to make it work.

Although the plot of *Make Lemonade* sounds like merely an adventure remembered by a young teen, the artful selection and arrangement of the imagery give the story a thematic coherence; Wolff's skill as an artist makes this book an emotionally powerful piece. One criterion used to determine if a literary piece is considered a work of art is whether or not it succeeds in evoking in the mind of the reader "vivid, lasting images that contribute to a feeling of possibility, even of believability" (Zitlow, 20). In an article that cites *Make Lemonade* as a young adult novel with particularly effective imagery, Connie Zitlow reviewed some of the novel's remarkable images selected by listeners and readers in her classes: "the astronaut left unconnected in space; all the dirt and filth; the small lemon seed and finally the sprouting lemon; the children, Jeremy and Jilly, described as leaking liquids everywhere" (Zitlow, 22). "Reading the highly-acclaimed book *Make Lemonade* . . . is like reading a picture" (Zitlow, 22).

One obvious image is the lemon of the title. Early on, while LaVaughn is still new to Jolly's life, she brings a pot of dirt and lemon seeds from her home. It is something that will grow into something "so beautiful you could have a nice day just from looking at it" (25). However, Jeremy is too young to understand the time it takes, so he parks himself in front of the pot to greet the plant when it comes. He sits there faithfully, expecting to see it grow. After a while, understandably, he gets angry and "thinks it's a lie" (76). LaVaughn wishes she could give him back his hope; more than anything, she wishes she could make his life easy. Her solution is to help Jeremy save many seeds so that they can grow a garden. They save oranges and a peach, and LaVaughn brings two more pots and more lemon seeds from home. When Jeremy plants the seeds, he looks like a child with no problems, a child whose life is as comfortable and predictable as the picture books with a mom and a dad and cookies in the oven (96). When Jolly and

LaVaughn fight, Jolly's last accusation, hurled to hurt LaVaughn most, is about the lemon seeds: "And you bring your phony little lemon seeds / they'll never bloom, / you're gonna break his heart!" (132). Next time, LaVaughn brings potting soil and fertilizer with her lemon seeds. It's not until the end of the book, after Jolly has saved her baby's life and doesn't need LaVaughn to babysit anymore, that she announces to her friend, "We got a little green thing / a little lemon thing comin' up" (199). Persistence has paid off.

Wolff also uses the image of the lemon to explain Jolly's ignorance and what she has made of the results. She tells the story of a poor blind woman who takes great pains to buy an orange for her children. On her way home, she is attacked and the orange is stolen from her. When one of the boys pretends to return it to her, she is grateful, thanking him for it before she stumbles home. Once home, she cuts it open, discovers that it's a lemon, and blames herself for being so stupid. At this point in the story, LaVaughn understands how Jolly has felt more stupid than angry; now she's angry at the boys who have seduced her and whom she has actually thanked. The story continues as the woman gets over her anger and makes lemonade from the lemon and a bit of sugar she has stored away. This is what Jolly can do; with a little help she can make lemonade from the lemons that her life has given her. Her anger gives her more energy and direction than did her desperation and fear. Now she can stop whining that nobody told her what to do, and begin doing for herself. Perhaps like LaVaughn's mother, she will become strong and capable. Wolff makes no promises; there are too many obstacles to make any valid predictions.

Hands are another motif that recurs throughout the book. While LaVaughn asks her mother for permission to babysit for Jolly, the two are making hamburger patties to store in the freezer. First they wash their hands together, as partners. As LaVaughn's mother mulls over the decision, her hands "shape the meat, slap it, lay it down" (18). When LaVaughn is deciding whether or not to accept this job, it is Jeremy's hand in hers that clinches her decision, and that is also what convinces her mother. By the time LaVaughn has babysat four times, her mind is "clenched like you'd clench a fist" (21). She had committed her time and energy to the two babies and to Jolly.

Hands comfort. When LaVaughn first misses school for a day because Jolly doesn't come home, her teacher gives her the assignments, and LaVaughn "thinks [she] feels her hand in the air / almost reaching for my shoulder / but I turn fast and go away / with the page numbers in my hand" (28). The clearest photo of LaVaughn and her parents before her father was shot has her small hand in his large one; the image brings back memories of security and good times to LaVaughn.

Hands can create. LaVaughn remembers the flower picture she put into her mother's big hands, hands that reminded her of her deceased father. She also remembers the approval of her mother, who recognizes her efforts: "Those hands did good work" (82). LaVaughn is learning that she is capable of accomplishing things of value in this world. It is a lesson Jolly has not had the opportunity to learn. LaVaughn passes on this essential lesson from her life to Jolly's son Jeremy. She teaches him how to use his hands to clean the floor and make his bed. "His hands are tough for pulling and lifting; / round little hands" (40). She is teaching him the self-respect that comes from creating order in one's life.

But hands can destroy, too. Jolly's boss seems to have more than two hands as he "put himself all over me" (57) in the back office. She defends herself by putting a pencil through his hand, and now she is fired with little recourse for justice or recompense.

Hands also communicate in other ways. When LaVaughn is trying to convince Jolly to be honest to Jeremy about planting lemon seeds, she holds her hands so stiffly like chicken wings that Jolly imitates her and dispels the impact of her seriousness with humor. One of the counselors "leans her arms in red sweater sleeves" on the desk as she talks, and then uses her hands to make a list "pulling her fingers down backwards one at a time / with the other hand" (126). LaVaughn notes that this gesture is common to teachers who like to instruct other people. She uses her hands to teach Jeremy his numbers, though he tends to focus on the number eleven, a number out of the reach of most hands.

Wolff's characters unfold through their body language. After Jolly gets hurt, LaVaughn's mother comes to help; "Jolly's eyes went undecided" (35), but then she lets her head float on the maternal shoulder. LaVaughn describes how they look when they visit the school: "Jeremy dancing his hacky sack dance, / Jolly shimmying her shimmy of / 'I got no problems . . . , Jilly bouncing on my arm" (91). LaVaughn's mom shrugs her shoulders as many mothers do, and she uses voices that LaVaughn imagines are part of the required training to be a mother.

Voices also serve as clues to character. When Jolly answers LaVaughn's initial telephone call, her voice sounds "like we could be friends" (4). Jilly's various ways of crying and Jeremy's speeches to the lemon pot are part of who they will be. Jeremy is internalizing LaVaughn's rules for living; she hears him passing them on to the objects in his environment. LaVaughn often wonders what Jilly is taking in, as she reacts only with her eyes. Wolff's success at imitating the wondrous range of expression of these two children comes from a well-developed sensitivity to the patterns of developing language, honed by many years of careful listening to voices, including those of her own children and grandchildren, and translating them into written language. Transmitting voices of young children onto a written page without making them sound overly cute or eager is not an easy task to achieve.

Some of Wolff's images are unique and deeply suggestive. A spider-web hangs above Jilly's highchair, as does the whole world of the spider, a world that Jilly can shake "just by her sad hollering" (22). LaVaughn is amazed at the impact of a mere infant, and conscious that her own actions can shake the world of Jolly and her two children. Jolly's essential loneliness and vulnerability are memorably clear in the image of a space explorer cut off from his spaceship by a door that closes and leaves him floating without a tether. Jeremy's clever imagination is indicated by the various hats he wears: LaVaughn's pocketbook when he is King of the Shoe Bus, and the pot lid he wears when he visits La Vaughn's house.

Another motif is Jolly's gift of humor; her ability to find laughter in almost any situation is what makes her an equal partner in her relationship with LaVaughn. LaVaughn sees this as her way of "taking hold, to make a joke out of a situation" (167). She remembers the fun they make of the television screen with no vertical hold, and the way they play the billionaire role when Jolly receives her reward of five dollars. Jolly can make fun of ridiculous questions in a math book or in the bureaucratic maze of an application, and even of all the blood that has flowed from women, year after year, into Mother Earth. Jolly's mere presence, with all her potential for toughness and humor, is what LaVaughn misses at the end of the book; she looks at Jolly with her "heart . . . so stretching like a room wanting company to come in, . . .

wanting to laugh at some joke with her / Any joke would have done" (199). LaVaughn has given so much love and care to Jolly and her children that she now recognizes what Jolly has given her in return and yearns for it. LaVaughn and Jolly have waded through the squalor to find a kind of love for each other that lasts. They have trusted each other and have honored that mutual trust. LaVaughn has worked without pay for Jolly, and Jolly has paid her back when she could, less with money than with the kind of courage that comes from deep within the gut, especially when Jolly returns to school and learns to persist. LaVaughn has defended Jolly against the scorn of her mother and friends, and Jolly has withheld her own resentment of LaVaughn's superiority and her successes with her children. They have forgiven each other after their fight, and now, at the end of their venture, when Jolly has taken hold of the structure that LaVaughn has helped her find, they let each other go.

The format of *Make Lemonade* looks like sixty-six narrative poems, each about two to four pages long. Wolff explains that she was writing neither free verse nor blank verse. "I'm not trying to write poetry. That would be very arrogant of me. I am not a poet. I wanted white space around the words, to feel more friendly to young moms who might not have time and concentration to read a lot of words all at one time" (Colburn, 3). In describing her preference for the poetic format of *Make Lemonade*, Wolff admits, "I myself am intimidated by huge pages of gray without any white space to thread through the story and give it room to breathe" (Sutton, 282).

"Actually, there's not a line of blank verse in either *Make Lemonade* or *True Believer*. Blank verse requires iambic pentameter, which I did not consciously use. However, I hope that the funny-shaped lines in which I wrote the book have a rhythm that approaches that of human speech, with the pauses, breathing spaces, confusions, and hesitations that we all have when we speak" (Gallo, 21). Wolff rebels against the oversimplification of the standard definition of a grammatical sentence as a group of words that express a complete thought. "What is a complete thought? 'Yikes! A bear!' or the story of Moses? Neither of those is exactly a sentence" (Gallo, 22). She describes her language as "units of thought" or "fragments of the things we try to say to each other in life. Sometimes they're only little squeaks of expression. I wrote those books that way in order to try to get as close as I could to the halting, gasping, sighing, shrugging, doubting, questioning way that we all speak" (Gallo, 22). She says that she "write[s] out loud" (Sutton, 282), speaking her lines over and over to make sure they sound natural. "LaVaughn, like her author, is never absolutely sure of what she's saying. Just as I am feeling my way through a narrative, La Vaughn is feeling her way through life" (Colburn, 3). LaVaughn is speaking in "the length of a breath" (Colburn, 3), and that is how she thinks and speaks, trying to make tangible her sensual memories of the smells and sounds and sights as much or more than her reflections back on the experience. She is trying to convey her experience more than her opinions about what happened.

"I wrote *Make Lemonade* as readers' theatre. I think it was the sound I was after" (Gallo, 21). This format brings together all of Wolff's talents and interests. Her musical experiences give her a sense of how words and sounds work, and how they could be phrased to make sense to the ear. Her interest in theatre inspires her to try on a wide variety of voices. After seeing Dustin Hoffman successfully don the guise of Shylock in Shakespeare's *Merchant of Venice*, Benjamin Braddock in *The Graduate*, Tootsie and Little Big Man in movies of the same names, she remembered an old ambition, inspired by watching a production of Luigi Pirandello's play *Six Characters in Search of an Author* in New York City shortly after her college days. Watching actors sitting on stools reading from scripts, she realized that she wanted to create and express the voices of different characters interacting. She wanted to write scripts of characters so rich that they would seem to live beyond the written story (Bowlan, 8). She has aspirations to use her art to perform on paper just as do actors onstage or behind cameras. On the other hand, Wolff has a horror of anything pretentious, such as dialogue in which a character seems self-conscious about the audience or language that seems written for the sake of its artfulness. Rather than identifying with a particular genre or style of writing, Wolff wants her readers to hear voices as authentically human as possible, and has expressed delight to hear that both *Make Lemonade* and *True Believer* have been staged as readings.

It is the tendency of readers to consider poetry pretentious that makes her leery of allowing people to call her work poetic. In an interview with Roger Sutton in *The Horn Book* magazine, the two discuss the differences between prose and poetry in relationship to *Make Lemonade* and *True Believer*. Sutton asserts that "to use a line break for dramatic effect, [and to use] . . . the shape of the page and the length of the lines to help tell the story," is to write poetry. Furthermore, he claims, Wolff is writing not just poetry but good-quality poetry in these two books because her language compresses meaning. "Poetry should have more *ergs* per word" (283), responded Wolff.

Sutton further points out that the test of whether a text is effective poetry or prose is to rearrange the lines into regular paragraphs. If the effect of the language changes, then the poetic lines are valid poetry. Wolff's two books pass that test. When her lines are rearranged, the meaning, rhythm, and impact of her language change; the structure of her prose, whether called poetry or not, has the impact of poetry. Besides the memorable imagery, the language itself has identifiable tempo, rhythm, and texture that are almost too subtle and changeable to define. Rereading *Make Lemonade* several times is like revisiting a piece of music in that the connections among the separate rhythms and motifs become more noticeable with familiarity.

On the one hand, the impact of this work is much more complex and far-reaching than most lyric poems, which compress meaning into an elegant concept or vision, and which leave a single memory, an image that sums up the essence of the poet's message. In contrast, Wolff's work leaves a plethora of images that keep reconnecting in memory into different patterns. As I reread and reconsider *Make Lemonade*, I keep discovering new aspects of the story. Long narrative poems also tell a story with a similar proliferation of suggestive and recurrent images that add thematic coherence. Most poetic narratives, however, describe an adventure with their heroic characters winning a clearly defined victory for the sake of a larger group. These differ from Wolff's works most obviously in scope and tone, but also in their endings. LaVaughn and Jolly have overcome obstacles but their victories are more ambiguous than other narratives. The shape of Wolff's plot is driven more by LaVaughn's memory than by a sequence of episodes. When Wolff is differentiating between a short story and a novel, she uses body language to make her point: "When I reach my arms way out to my sides and then bend them upward, I can encompass a short story. . . . But with my arms in that position I can't possibly reach around [a novel]" (Singer, 38). This is not a book that is easily bound by either gesture.

Other young adult novels use a similar stylistic format. Karen Hesse's *Out of the Dust*, Brenda Seabrooke's *Judy Scuppernong*, and Robert Cormier's *Frenchtown Summer* are included in a list along with *Make Lemonade* of "Verse Novels for YAs" compiled in 1999 by Jonathan Hunt. Perhaps these novels that look like poetry and use appropriate imagistic language are examples of a new form of literature. They divide their story into slices or pieces that mimic the way we learn about other people and new fields of experiences, one bit of information or one scene at a time.

Readers have reacted well to *Make Lemonade*. Some letters to Wolff have claimed that the book helps them empathize with people from different backgrounds, especially in its sensitive treatment of the plight of single teenage mothers. The warm public reaction has given Wolff opportunities to travel, speak at conferences, and meet new people. She is keenly aware of the irony that her chance to "get all dressed up and eat expensive food with interesting people in distant cities" contrasts immensely with the lives of her impoverished subjects (Gallo, 5). While writing *Make Lemonade*, she became aware of a deeply held conviction: "It's criminal for children to have to live surrounded by ugliness. I didn't know I knew that till I could really *see* the absence of beauty" (Wolff, 9). Enriched by much beauty in her own life, Wolff had to imagine deeply to describe lives so barren of easy loveliness.

One of the reactions Wolff did not appreciate is the assumption by many readers that the characters in *Make Lemonade* are African-American. She did not intend that her characters be any particular race or ethnic group. Rather, Wolff hoped that readers would "have the characters be whatever ethnicity they *needed* them to be" (Sutton, 281). One reader has sent her a picture where the characters are obviously Asian. My students in Appalachia thought the characters sounded "country," even though they might be living in an urban area. Other students assume that the characters are white or black or Hispanic. Wolff was disappointed that some adult librarians and critics keep placing the characters and setting in an African-American environment. "I didn't see faces so much as I heard voices when I was writing. I think we do our best writing when we get out of the way and let our charac-

Wolff's grandson Max, age ten, in her home.

ters speak in whatever voices they have to speak in" (Zvirin, 1251). Wolff feels that it would be as false and as arrogant to write in "black" talk as it would have been to talk Irish or Italian. "I am extremely white" (Zvirin, 1251), she says. She has lived and taught in enough cities to talk young and to talk urban poor, but she refuses to claim the voice of any particular ethnic group.

Their ethnic identities seem to be of less concern to most young readers than to adult critics. Wolff was actually trying to write a raceless story, following the dream of Martin Luther King that "there would be a time when his children would be judged not by the color of their skin, but by the content of their character" (Colburn, 3). She is grateful that her editor, Brenda Bowen, let her publish a book that not only used "funny-shaped lines" but omitted the last names of the characters, their ethnicity, and the name of the city where they lived. Could she get away with that? Apparently so. However, Wolff did respond to the assumptions and questions about racial tensions in this book by following *Make Lemonade* with *Bat 6*, which deals explicitly with a racial issue.

Another question that arises is about the setting. How is Wolff able to write about a place so different from her rural home in Oregon? She responds that inner-city life was so foreign to the scenery of her youth that her first experiences in an urban setting made an unusually strong impact on her. When her own children were infants, she lived in a Queens apartment very similar to that of LaVaughn's home. Her own children were as "sloppy, drippy [and] adorable" as those of Jolly (Colburn, 2). Wolff relates to the characters in other ways too. For much of her life she had shared with Jolly a sense of appearing inept to the people around her. She has felt the same loneliness and fear of the future, but also Jolly's keen sense of the ridiculous. LaVaughn's impulsive decisions are familiar to Wolff as "she too, lurches from mistake to mistake" (Colburn, 2). To admirers of Wolff's artistic successes, her mistakes are invisible. What is obvious is her empathy for people who struggle hard to achieve a life of goodness and beauty. Whether or not each detail of the story she is telling can be matched up with a lived experience, Wolff has grasped the authentic language that makes her story viscerally realistic. That quality of her work has garnered the enthusiastic support of many readers as well as critics.

In its year of publication, 1993, the merit of *Make Lemonade* was recognized immediately with a wide variety of awards. *The School Library Journal* named it a Best Book of the Year. It made *Booklist*'s "Top of the List." It won the Parent's Choice Book Award, the Bank Street Child Study Book Award, and the Oregon Book Award for Young Readers, and the *Bulletin for the Center for Children's Books* designated it as a Blue Ribbon Book. In 1994 it won more awards, including the Michigan Library Association's Thumbs Up! Award for YA Fiction, a Golden Kite Award, and a YALSA Best Book for Young Adults. In 2000, Swiss student readers selected it for the Preiselbär Award, and in 2002, it was named a YALSA Popular Paperback for Young Adults. Fortunately for readers and critics, Wolff decided to continue tracing the lives of *Make Lemonade*'s characters. *True Believer* picks up their story a year later.

References

Colburn, Nell. "The Incomparable Wolff," *School Library Journal* 48, no. 2 (February 2002): 54–56.

Gallo, Don. "Virginia Euwer Wolff." Interview. Authors4Teens.com. http://www.authors4teens.com/A4T?source=interview&authorid=wolff (16 Jan. 2001).

Hughes-Hassell, Sandra, and Sandy L. Guild. "The Urban Experience in Recent Young Adult Novels." *The ALAN Review* 29, no. 3 (Spring/Summer 2002): 35–39.

Hunt, Jonathan. "Verse Novels for YAs." www.seemore.mi.ort/booklists/VerseNovels.txt (3 Jan. 2002).

Nobles, Susanne. "Why Don't We Ever Read Anything Happy?" *The ALAN Review* 26, no. 3 (Fall 1998): 46–50.

Salinger, J. D. "For Esmé—With Love and Squalor," *Nine Stories*. Bantam Books, 1948, 1981. 87–114.

Singer, Marilyn. "What Is a Short Story?" *The ALAN Review* 28, no. 1 (Fall 2000): 38-40.

Sutton, Roger. "An Interview with Virginia Euwer Wolff," *The Horn Book* 77, no. 3 (May/June 2001): 280–288.

"Virginia Euwer Wolff." AuthorChats (5 Dec. 2001). http://www.authorchats.com/archives/viewArchive.jsp?id=20011205VirginiaEuwerWolff.jsp (7 Oct. 2002).

Wolff, Virginia. "What we Lose, What we Find." Speech presented at The ALAN Breakfast Meeting, National Council of Teachers Conference, Atlanta, Ga., 23 Nov. 2002.

Zitlow, Connie S. "Sounds and Pictures in Words: Images in Literature for Young Adults," *The ALAN Review* 27, no. 1 (Winter 2000): 20–26.

Zvirin, Stephanie. "The Booklist Interview: Virginia Euwer Wolff," *Booklist*, 1 (Mar. 1994): 1250–1251.

CHAPTER 6

~

True Believer:
Living with Faith

On November 22, 1963, Virginia Euwer Wolff was feeding her daughter lunch in a highchair when she heard that President Kennedy had been shot. This highchair would surface in her memory as she was beginning to conceive her novel *Make Lemonade* (Wolff 2002). Reaction by readers to what they perceived as ethnic qualities in *Make Lemonade* instigated Wolff's next writing project, *Bat 6*, about how an act of racial hatred sent shock waves of self-doubt about the moral harmony in two small towns in rural America. After World War II, many traditional institutions seemed outdated and too simple for those returning from war, who had seen life outside of the rural U.S. and had met people from other cultures with different values. The last half of the twentieth century saw a questioning of most values, proprieties, and assumptions that had seemed to define American life up until then. And then there came the terrorist attack of September 11, 2001. The boundaries that defined what was safe and secure are once again pulled down. What happens now?

Many people have felt afraid since then; their trust in the American systems of protection from war and want has been irretrievably damaged. Even Virginia Euwer Wolff, who won such acclaim for *Make Lemonade* and spent so much time and effort in exploring issues of resiliency, has admitted that she stopped writing for a while. By the time of the terrorist attack on the World Trade Center, *True Believer* had been published and was on the way to earning the National Book Award for 2001. Although the timing of the choice was probably coincidental, the book's attempt to show the way out of despair and distrust was most apt in addressing the nation's mood. Like most writers for young people, Wolff worries about what kind of book to write in the aftermath of these terrible and sudden attacks on symbols of American strength. Much of the work she has already written, including *Make Lemonade* and *True Believer* is appropriate literature for readers who are experiencing depression and despair. Instead of preaching a particular set of beliefs, she simply portrays young people who continue to strive throughout their most discouraging days, working hard and persistently to understand and sometimes even forgive the people they care about. They strive to live, even through what they do not yet comprehend or believe; they strive to hope for one more perception of beauty or moment of laughter.

Wolff had not planned to write a sequel to *Make Lemonade*, but she kept thinking about Jolly and LaVaughn and wondering what was going to happen next. She was very aware of the dangers of writing a sequel, especially to a book with such a warm reception as *Make Lemonade*. In an interview with Roger Sutton of *The Horn Book* magazine, she agreed with *Booklist* critic Hazel Rochman that the "best books make you *want* a sequel but refuse to give it to you" (281). Good books have changed your viewpoint forever, and they keep reminding you of something new to consider. Wolff realized that *True Believer* might be "pedestrian and mediocre, two of the sins in [her] church" (281). Even with these trepidations, she found herself delighted to be working again with LaVaughn and Jolly. "I loved being back with that family. I was rejoining my friends. I felt they were unfinished" (Bowlan, 8). And she found that writing in the "funny-shaped lines" freed her from the constraints of traditionally normal prose fiction. Moreover, when dealing with the dialect of her inner-city characters, this method of writing seems to highlight the musical rhythms and special intensities of their oral language.

True Believer focuses more on LaVaughn than on Jolly. One of its important themes has its source in the movie *Thelma and Louise*: "'You get what you settle for'" (Bowlan, 10). When Wolff heard this line, she says "it went to my spine"; it rang true to her own life, and she decided to include it as a central part of LaVaughn's story. When Wolff began to

write *Make Lemonade*, she focused on Jolly, and LaVaughn existed more
as a shadowy character whose supportive role was to witness and reflect
on Jolly's burdens, and then to tell the story. But Wolff's editor, Brenda
Bowen, suggested that she fill in LaVaughn's background, so Wolff
typed out an interview with her: "What do you like to do? What are
your hobbies?" (*Publishers' Weekly*, 1). She claims that the character in
her head seemed to resent that she was being treated as an after-
thought, but she finally evolved as a complete person with all the
quirky opinions and habits of a real and complex individual.

Wolff has often referred to her slowness as a writer and thinker,
though few YA authors have written as many works that are so thoroughly considered and so intricately crafted. Although Wolff spent
three years writing *Make Lemonade*, it was the fastest book she had
written and published up to that time. Its sequel, *True Believer*, was
written in only two years. It had taken Wolff a whole eight months to
find a name for the narrator of the *Make Lemonade* series, as it is now
called. "I knew one would come to me, and one did. Verna LaVaughn
got two names, my attempt to recompense her for having to wait so
long" (Gallo, 1). As mentioned before, the actual source for the name
Verna is Wolff's first grade teacher. LaVaughn was actually the name of
the owner of a beauty shop in Wolff's hometown. Although some critics have considered the name typically African-American, Wolff explains that her sources for the names are "very white."

In the beginning of *True Believer* the two names are attributed to the
two aunts who have raised LaVaughn's mother. Now somewhat elderly,
they exemplify the rigorous rectitude that has been passed down
through LaVaughn's mother. To a large extent, LaVaughn's experiences
with Jolly soften the edges that distinguish the territory of right from all
the bad and dangerous behaviors in the neighborhood. Now
LaVaughn's mother seems to be softening too, as she begins to spend
time with a man. La Vaughn is trying to shape her own definitions of
right and wrong. While she still intends to succeed in school, get into
college, and leave the neighborhood of dangerous poverty, she also
yearns for romantic experience.

The traditional view of American teenage years is that they are the
best time of life, but Wolff agrees with Ursula LeGuin whom she quotes
as lamenting "Adolescence is exile" (Wolff 2002, 9). At the beginning of

this subsequent novel, LaVaughn is more sure of herself than at the beginning of *Make Lemonade*. She asserts herself positively: "My name is LaVaughn and I am 15" (3). She also describes herself as more complex and full of questions. How do you avoid getting hurt by teenage romance? She doesn't want to hate men; she wants love, but how do you recognize true love?

For now, though, she is confident that her path ahead is full of promise. She has good friends, Myrtle and Annie, whom she has known for most of her life. They are loyal to each other and familiar with each other's problems. Myrtle's father slumps in and out of drug rehab programs; the girls know not to ask about this shadowy figure who stares at the television screen when he is home. Annie, who has had several stepfathers, is not too sure what will happen next. The three friends keep a united front against the dangerous alleys that "reek / . . . full of deadly events that could happen any moment" (14). They trust each other to be a refuge of stability in a world of unexpected change.

LaVaughn has a room of her own. She is an only child in a family that loves her. True, her father died when she was young, but LaVaughn has no doubt that she is valued and loved. She has so much ownership of her room that she paints a tree with a nest of birds on her wall. This expression of her individual vision on the wall of their rented apartment first shocks her mother, but she only expresses her pleasure. "Your father would be proud" (16), she says, and LaVaughn will always value that generous comment. LaVaughn's mother accepts a new job that will take more effort and time but also earn more money, and that will help pay for LaVaughn to go to college. Her dream is to see her daughter escape this world of drug-related accidents, enforced pregnancy, and dead-end dreams. When LaVaughn, at the age of ten, first mentions the idea of attending college, her mother takes hold of the idea as a possible route out of the neighborhood.

LaVaughn does her part by faithfully finishing her homework and paying attention to what the teachers say in class. It is hard to pay attention, however, in classes where the kids make too many jokes and too much noise. But LaVaughn strains to hear; she and her mother have painted a makeshift bookshelf in her room where she keeps all her books, including a dictionary she has bought. At the instigation of one of those teachers who takes the time to notice and encourage individual students, LaVaughn starts attending an after-school class to improve her grammar.

Although she shuns didactic writing, Wolff is too much the teacher to avoid completely the urge to give her characters good advice. In *Make Lemonade* LaVaughn's mother warns her daughter to complete all her homework and never to use the word "ain't." Jolly knows about the dangers of seeking help from Welfare Services, but LaVaughn keeps seeking until she finds a program connected with a school. Again and again LaVaughn quotes her mother about the importance of hard work, persistence, and saving money. Wonderful teachers often play a vital role in opening doors for LaVaughn to leave the poverty and pain of her neighborhood. Wolff portrays them as gatekeepers who watch their students with care and use thoughtfully chosen words to counsel them.

The final section of *Make Lemonade* opens with Jolly beginning school in the Moms Up program where her children can attend daycare, and LaVaughn hears advice from her fourth-period teacher, who has noticed the "discontent" in her face and suggests that she prepare to attend college by attending a class in leadership skills, a workshop for financial aid, and, finally, a course called Grammar Build-Up. "And believe me, you need it. I have high hopes for you / But your grammar frankly stinks" (118). Like all good teachers, she knows how to soften a true but painful assessment with an accompanying gesture of kindness. At the beginning of the next semester, she reminds LaVaughn of this advice, squeezing through a crowded hall to give her an explicit push into the class. Good teachers can be a pain in the neck to students until they fulfill their promise.

Wolff describes the two main teachers in LaVaughn's life as tall, perhaps not just in physical height, but in the way they loom in their students' minds. One day the teacher of the Steam Class "wears nests of rings" (88), a purple dress and running shoes; the next day a bright orange sweater—obviously a person confident enough to express her individual style with flair. The teacher acts with sensitivity and subtle power; she knows how to demand courtesy from her students. Wolff's lessons focus on enumerating strengths (or "capables"), practicing assertive behavior, and establishing boundaries so nobody gets too close or keeps too far away.

In *True Believer*, the most prominent teacher is Dr. Rose, who teaches different ways to use the English language in a volunteer after-school program called Grammar Build-Up. Wolff claims to love this character. She builds a lesson for her on a line from the poet Ellen Bryant Voigt, who once said in a lecture, "Adjectives qualify the world" (Sutton, 284). In *True Believer*, Dr. Rose says, "Nouns name the world. Adjectives qualify it. Verbs are our meager attempt to record the vast motion of all life; prepositions connote the relationship among phenomena" (38).

Ever the English teacher, Wolff, through the character of Dr. Rose, reminds readers about the difference between "lie" and "lay" and when to use "whom"—not once but often enough to be effective teaching. As LaVaughn takes hold of grammar in the class, she reminds herself throughout the day to use correct grammar, and she begins to notice the grammatical quirks of others, even her mother.

Dr. Rose teaches more than grammar. A woman of great self-possession who dresses with elegance equal to her speech, she preaches self-respect and high aspirations. Speaking slowly and deliberately, she notes that this one percent of the school population "will become taller / should you choose to remain" (40). She urges her students to believe that language can improve their lives:

> Remember, our goal is lucidity.
> Gleaming lucidity.
> Only when we are lucid can we be constructive.
> Only when we are constructive
> can we live with good conscience in the world.
> Only when we live with good conscience in the world
> will the rage of the people calm. (171)

Through Dr. Rose, Wolff suggests that before accomplishing anything worthwhile for the world, we need to use language to shape our thoughts and perceptions so clearly that we can be confident in their truth. We need to question and clarify our ideas until only their elegant essence remains. Carving out of our language all the unnecessary connotations and implications that might be misunderstood takes long hard work, and that is another truth that Wolff demonstrates in the teaching of Dr. Rose.

Dr. Rose organizes her classes into drill groups with a precision that lets her students know that this is serious business. LaVaughn's group makes a game of the drills, wearing hats for motivation and giving themselves the name "Brain Cells" for mutual support. Using standard grammar correctly signals a precise understanding of the structure of language, and that is powerful in positions of leadership. It commands respect from teachers, bosses, and other professionals. This is a class that lifts LaVaughn's spirit.

Grammar Build-Up is not the only door that is opening for LaVaughn. The school suddenly recognizes LaVaughn as potentially college-bound, so they move her from the science class she shares with Myrtle and Annie to a biology class. She has never seen the material in the book, and the new vocabulary is daunting. The other students look "unfamiliar. Even their hair conditioner smells different" (55). Fortunately for LaVaughn, her lab partner, who is also new to the class, is a whiz at understanding biology and can explain to her how all these new facts relate to each other. LaVaughn feels fortunate to be a part of this rarefied atmosphere. She is amazed at the good condition of the equipment and the quiet in the room that lets the teacher be heard. She agrees with her partner Patrick that science is beautiful.

Besides school, another piece of LaVaughn's plan is to earn money. She finds a job in the laundry at the Children's Hospital where she folds and delivers sheets, and where she also has a chance to talk with the children who show so much courage as they undergo treatment for serious illnesses. She begins to think that she would like to work as a nurse.

LaVaughn's life seems to be going according to plan; she feels as if she is on the right track for achieving her goals. At this point, her "hope is strong like an athlete" (14). To top it all off, a childhood pal returns to the building and he is gorgeous.

Jody is smart and beautiful, and he too wants to attend college. When LaVaughn recognizes him in the elevator, her heart starts a life of its own and she finds it difficult to speak. "My heart is so full of heartbeats it jolts my thinking" (23). Jody and LaVaughn had played kick-the-can and card games as children. Their mothers shared a close bond, especially after the death of LaVaughn's father. The two had traded keys and given them to their children in case of an emergency. Jody's mother had moved them away to a better neighborhood where she cleaned houses in order to give her son more opportunities. Through one of her wealthy employers, Jody has learned about competitive swimming, and now he travels across town to swim in a pool that he keeps clean in return. But his mother has now returned them to this neighborhood exhausted and discouraged; she has been unable to pay the higher rent in a better neighborhood. "You be nice to Jody, LaVaughn," says her mother. "They don't have it easy" (25). So enamored of Jody's perfect body is LaVaughn that the idea of sympathizing with him seems ludicrous. She agrees to be nice, her face "flat as a plate, no expression" (25). Jody is all that LaVaughn can think about. When they meet in the elevator, he jokes with her and gives her an orange. LaVaughn decides that he is the last piece in her life plan. Her dream is that they will go to college, marry, and enjoy their cute children.

Then shadows begin to fall on LaVaughn's bright new world. Myrtle and Annie are increasingly engaged in a new church club, the Joyful Universal Church of Jesus. They keep inviting LaVaughn to join, but the group's tendency to relegate people into separate exclusive compartments, either good or evil, bothers LaVaughn, as does their tendency to insist they know the only answers to life's problems. For LaVaughn, their answers are too simple to seem valid. For example, they solve the confusing issue of how to stay virgin during adolescence by joining the club "Cross Your Legs for Jesus" (5). Memorizing Bible verses and participating in carefully chaperoned coed events seem harmless, but LaVaughn doesn't agree with blaming the victims of rape or condemning people who make mistakes. Myrtle and Annie are horrified that LaVaughn accepts the theory of evolution she learns in biology class. They invite her to a drama in which Jesus systematically destroys characters representing a drug addict, a knifer, a drinker, a girl who has had an abortion, and a homosexual. LaVaughn is puzzled that her friends have adopted such extreme views.

Then her widowed mother begins to date a man, and, for the first time in LaVaughn's memory, seems to flirt. She knows that her mother loved her husband. Pictures of him are everywhere, and only good memories remain. Certainly, after endless hard work and sacrifices, her mother deserves to enjoy someone else, and Lester seems nice enough. Still, LaVaughn can hardly keep from resenting him out of loyalty to her father. Everything he says seems either too affected or silly, and her mother disgusts her by putting on airs. Out of respect for her mother, LaVaughn is polite, and she does realize that her mother enjoys a man's appreciation after all these years. Mostly LaVaughn is lonely as she retires to her room and thinks about Jody. She is sure that her father, Guy, would bring her and Jody together.

The classes at school are difficult, but LaVaughn floats through, her mind focused on the upcoming Food and Flashlight Formal. She dreams of going together with Jody as her first date, and it would be perfect. But Patrick asks her first. He is too nice, too willing to carry her books, and too eager to help her in biology. He talks slowly and he seems to own only two shirts. LaVaughn cannot help herself; she refuses his invitation by telling him what she hopes is true. She claims to be going with someone else.

Jody, however, is still a mystery. He is friendly to her, but doesn't seem as excited to see her as she is to see him. Mostly he is ambitious to get out of the neighborhood. That keeps him swimming and studying as hard as he can. He seems unconscious of the dance. Instead, Jody invites her to the pool to help him practice life-saving moves. LaVaughn's figure looks good in the swimsuit she has borrowed from Myrtle because it is newer. She knows that from Jody's initial surprise when he sees her. Immediately, he detaches himself; his face closes "like a tablecloth coming down over a table" (76). All the touching and swimming thrill LaVaughn, but afterward, Jody is still removed; he talks about his earnest desire to know how to save a life someday, and then he tells her she can go home. LaVaughn is jolted. "Jody touches my life by touching me / and he says I can go home" (80). To Jody, LaVaughn is a pal, but she wants more.

Finally, LaVaughn takes matters into her own hands and asks Jody to the dance. He agrees: "Sure, why not?" LaVaughn is ecstatic. "My first date ever. / My brain is full of that dress / and enough imagination to cover the planet" (82). She has so much imagination that she hasn't noticed how casual Jody is.

They have a wonderful time dancing and singing along with all the others, laughing and singing the same silly song over and over, and flashing their lights at ten. Jody walks her to the door and thanks her for making him go to the dance. "It was fun." LaVaughn's imagination has been planning this moment for almost two weeks: "You could kiss me, Jody" (87). This is the first kiss that she has yearned for, even before she knew that Jody had returned to the neighborhood. But it doesn't happen. Jody brushes her lips with his, just pretending to kiss and, softly, laughs, "just a bit of a chuckle" (87). Then he walks off.

LaVaughn is staggered. Her dream is coming apart. How can she marry Jody if she isn't even good enough for a kiss? What could be so wrong about her? The only person she can discuss this with is Jolly, but they immediately lapse into their old pattern of chatter and complaints. LaVaughn is suspicious of Jolly's boast that her new boyfriend has taught Jeremy to read, but the little boy proves her wrong. She does not have a chance to discuss Jody. Jody is in her mind, but she doesn't see or hear from him until she lets herself into his apartment and props a photo against his fish tank. Tiptoeing into his bedroom, she leans down and smells his pillow. She forgives his lack of a kiss; maybe it is his first kiss too. When she gets his note thanking her four days later, the tone is not particularly romantic: "Thanks for the pic. Where are you Buddy?" (117). But LaVaughn carries the note around next to her heart. When she meets him on the elevator after a shooting and expresses concern, she is ready to fall into his arms, but he closes down like an island. Strangest of all is Patrick's comment when he sees Jody's name on her notebook. "Then it's not your boyfriend" (135). LaVaughn is confused. How can she be so passionate and everyone not know?

Other parts of her life seem confusing too. Her mother and Lester, the man she is dating, begin to discuss moving to a house in a safer part of the city. LaVaughn tries to show respectful interest, but all she can think of is that she will miss Jody. When she tells Jody, he agrees that he will miss her too. He is obviously fond of his old pal LaVaughn, but she is nonplussed at their lack of warmth and connection.

LaVaughn recognizes her good fortune in being placed in advanced classes that will make her eligible for college, but she is also aware that these changes are separating her from her past. The Grammar Build-Up class is a source of new friends. The etymology of grammar links it to "glamour," from a time when expertise in using language seemed magical, especially to a populace where that expertise was scarce. But in many public school hallways, grammatical precision is anathema; it seems to offend the principle of democracy, equal opportunity for all classes, regardless of their language skills. As LaVaughn begins to speak with more precision and correctness, her friends Myrtle and Annie accuse her of becoming a snob. Patrick is offended when LaVaughn corrects his language. Part of improving one's language is learning how to adapt to social conventions of the privileged, and this world may seem uppity to those who are not learning how to unlock those doors.

When her friends make these accusations, LaVaughn is shattered with guilt and sorrow. Then her new friends in Grammar Build-Up remind her that this is the price she must pay for wanting to improve her lot. Her friends and family may not know how to accept this part of her; she must learn to accept them as they are. Some of the students have lost friends who want to keep them from entering and rising toward another social stratum. Others have been luckier and kept friends who only tease them about their improved language and manners.

The worst happens when she discovers that Jody's romantic feelings are focused on someone else. LaVaughn has decided to surprise Jody with a plate full of chocolate chip cookies and the pictures from the dance. Using her key, she walks into his apartment and sees the silhouette of two boys kissing. One is Jody. Now she knows beyond a doubt that he has been at most a fond friend to her, and that is all he will continue to be. After weeks of obsessing about her love for Jody, LaVaughn crashes. How could she not have known? Annie had accused him of being strange; Patrick has been so sure that Jody could not be her boyfriend, and she herself now remembers Jody's grief when his friend Victor had gotten involved with drugs and been killed by a gunshot, shortly before he and his mother had left the neighborhood.

But are these clues to Jody's lack of passion for her? Wolff carefully doesn't address the question of whether LaVaughn should have known that Jody was gay, or whether he should have told her, or whether he even knew it himself. These questions are left to hang unanswered in the reader's mind. The focus of Wolff's novel is the depth of LaVaughn's shock and despair. The floor has been pulled from beneath her.

The day after her discovery she feels like a large rock embedded in heavy clay, unable to move. Her mother, however, not knowing the cause or the extent of her despair, and despising self-indulgence, forces her to go to school. LaVaughn thinks she now understands "the walking suicide kids" (200); she feels like disappearing; she is in shock. Her mind doesn't work and her grades go down. Her life seems a tragedy, a brief painful moment on earth with no meaning and no hope but an unpredictable death.

Then the guidance counselor calls her in; the school personnel are concerned at the drop in her grades. "LaVaughn, do you want to go to college?" he asks. Out of habit LaVaughn agrees that she does want to go to college; the habitual words spark her into hopefulness. Perhaps she could be a nurse: The counselor perks up; he is interested to hear about her dreams. Encouraged by his attention, LaVaughn spills out all her experiences at the hospital, realizing as she talks that wanting to go to college means that she hasn't yet finished living her life. The guidance counselor invites her to a career tour of the nursing school, and this offer lifts up her spirit. The next morning she apologizes to Patrick for hurting his feelings and he relents; they work together again. Her mother has stopped dating Lester, and there is no more talk of leaving the neighborhood. Bravely LaVaughn tells her mother about her heart that feels broken and cries out her sorrow on her mother's shoulder.

Puzzled by her transition from despair to hope, and prompted by the religious signs she sees around her and the comments of Myrtle and Annie, LaVaughn decides to explore the question of religion. It was easier than thinking about her own problems. Myrtle has told her that she is getting "too good for Jesus" (176), and then they hesitate about coming to her party because they are supposed to limit their contact with non-Christians. "It's too hard for God to get through / when there's clutter. Non-Christians are distracting" (241). What kind of religion is this?

Many adolescents explore religious creeds and moral codes as they compare the traditions they have learned from their families with new information and experiences. This questioning is particularly true of American youth who have been entrenched in a culture so self-conscious of religious differences that its government regulates the separation of church and state. In many areas of the country, religious affiliation defines a person's social connections. LaVaughn thus seems particularly American in seeking out information about the religious beliefs of her friends and family. Myrtle and Annie have relegated their moral decision-making to a higher authority. In contrast, LaVaughn seems more representative of the democratic tendency to honor individuals by merit rather than by accident of birth and connection. Like the minister she meets at a church near the hospital where she works, LaVaughn tends to be more inclusive, less judgmental.

During the twentieth century, the rising domination of scientific thought, which seeks a truth logically deduced from observed phenomena, caused many to question the definitions of truth based only on traditional or institutional power. Perhaps in reaction to the increasing dependence on science and technology for answers, there seems to be a revival of spirituality and interest in religion. One example is Pentecostalism, one of the world's fastest growing religious movements, which claims a fourth of the world's Christians, or 450 million people. Based on fervent experiences of spiritual emotion and aggressively evangelical, and emphasizing spiritual sustenance in the here and now, it nurtures people who don't find the traditional formalized and intellectualized religions fulfilling. Followers of the Pentecostal movement don't have a creed or a hierarchy; each believer receives direction from his or her personal experience of the Spirit. This sincere immediacy seems to be the religious tendency of Manzanita in Wolff's *Bat 6*. As fervent a believer and as generous as she is with her efforts and time, however, she makes no effort to convert anyone to her own way of relating to God. She seems to have no interest in exercising power over others except to perform what she feels is God's will. Perhaps Wolff means to contrast Manzanita's personal faith and private inspirations, which she uses only to direct her own actions, with the evangelical urgency of Myrtle and Annie, who spend most of their efforts in condemning others.

Wolff's own religious background was directed by her mother's faithful participation in the town's Presbyterian church: "My mother was a religious force. She was a church organist, and I went to Sunday school and church my whole childhood" (Colburn, 2). As a teenager, Wolff attended an Episcopal boarding school where courses in church history and religion were required. She remembers the chaplain, Father Evan Williams, as an important mentor who responded enthusiastically to her questioning of the Christian traditions they were studying in a church history class as well as those she had absorbed throughout her childhood. She remembers probing for answers about the purpose of human existence, about God, and about the nature of good and evil, questions that recur particularly in *Bat 6*, *Make Lemonade*, and *True Believer*. In college, Wolff took a class in Eastern religions which expanded her view of how faith could be defined in a broader cultural spectrum. Wolff has remained interested in diverse expressions of religious faith. Her son Anthony has a degree in religious studies and has shared his exploration of various religious philosophies and rituals.

In writing *True Believer*, Wolff differentiates between strong belief and fundamentalism: "fundamentalists are different from others pursuing the religious quest [in that] they are so sure they're right" (Colburn, 2). Fundamentalists seem to need a single answer that will encompass all the questions that they ask. Often they seem to resent or be suspicious of any questions that stretch their definition of right and wrong. This simple, sharply defined view of the world often keeps them from seeing the humor in many instances of human frailty. A sense of humor stems from a generous worldview that recognizes with laughter the limitations of strict definitions. While some humor, of course, is cruel and judgmental of those who are different, good-natured humor indicates a fundamental humility and modesty about one's own cultural conventions and allows for other possibilities of truth. Fundamentalists often react with fear and anger at any sense that their conception of the world's structure may not work for all people and all situations.

In *Bat 6*, Shazam has learned this fearful fundamentalist thinking from her mother, who repeatedly abuses and abandons her. She has taught Shazam that all people of Japanese descent are evil; they murdered her father in the Pearl Harbor attack. She doesn't listen to her classmates' stories about their friendly Japanese-American neighbors, nor does she question her mother's fearsome stereotype when she plays ball with Aki, a view too simple to let in experience: Be afraid of Japanese faces. Only when Manzanita forces her to acknowledge the injury she has inflicted does she begin to regret it and open herself to friendship with Aki's brother.

Wolff differentiates between the strict fundamentalism of Shazam and of LaVaughn's friends Myrtle and Annie, and the more open-minded humility and spirituality of those who are certain of their own experience of God. Manzanita knows that she has heard God's voice directly, but she doesn't impose her beliefs on others. She is confident that God speaks directly to her, and in times of crisis she prays directly, without inserting her opinion about what should be done. Though confident in her faith, she is utterly humble in expressing that faith to others. Manny's experiences of God do not give her a sense of power over any other human. While she is directing Shazam to do what she believes is necessary, she apologizes to God for her bossiness and hopes for His forgiveness. While wholly open to the emotional and even physical manifestations of experiencing God's word, Manny is sensible and logical in the actions she undertakes for His sake.

LaVaughn juxtaposes her scientific knowledge against the religion of Myrtle and Annie; they seem to believe in the literal numbers and words of the Bible, while LaVaughn believes the truth of scientific information with as much certainty. Not until Patrick articulates the difference between the language of the Bible as story and the language of science as fact are their arguments put into suitable perspective.

So what, finally, does LaVaughn "truly with all [her] heart believe"? Dr. Rose has suggested that what the school needs "to believe in thoroughly [is] . . . that you . . . can stand up tall, shatter those statistics / about students in the 'poorer schools,' as they call us, / and make a difference in the vast / and terrifying and magnificent world" (170). Gaining this confidence in her work sustains LaVaughn until she loses her romance with Jody and falls into a ditch of depression. What lifts her out are her caring teachers who ask why her grades are falling and set up an appointment with a guidance counselor. The counselor listens carefully enough to elicit from LaVaughn that she wants to be a nurse, and then he does something about it: He sets up a career tour for her. LaVaughn is lifted up enough to begin to mend her life. She asks a truculent Patrick for forgiveness, and she tries to reconnect with Myrtle and Annie. In questioning the meaning of life beyond the life-and-death cycle, she wonders about religions. Like many young people, she isn't so interested in the differences among doctrines or the habits of various institutions; she wants to know how to link her daily experiences with spiritual motivation. What keeps a person going? How does a person cope with tragedy and loss? What or who is God?

She also inquires about the cross Patrick wears. To him it acts as a reminder that "evil's always gonna be around, / and you deal with it" (220). Her other friends are more uncertain about God and church, accusing institutionalized religions of causing dissension and instigating war. Although LaVaughn's mother has stopped going to church, she depends on God for the strength to raise her child. When LaVaughn talks to a neighborhood minister, she learns about another kind of religion, where God welcomes everyone, regardless of who they are or what they have done. "We weren't put on Earth to exclude each other," he says. In contrast, he defines Hell as "when we stop caring about each other. We wouldn't wish that on anyone" (228). This is a generous definition of religion, and it pleases LaVaughn. "Religion must be for trusting. / And trusting, what is that for? / I figured it out: It helps you go on / when you can't go on" (236). Sometimes it is difficult to know exactly what to trust. LaVaughn has trusted her emotional response to Jody and assumed the sexual attraction she was feeling was mutual. When she finds her passion was one-sided, embarrassment so floods her mind that she feels her life is almost not worth living. Trusting that her horrible feelings will change, that something good will happen, and that she will survive and perhaps even succeed is the very general definition of religion that LaVaughn now feels. It is a certainty of hope; she has faith in "the possibility of possibility. Of the world making sense someday" (243). "I'm a true believer. / And that's a fact." Wolff chose her title as she was considering the values that LaVaughn chooses to believe and to uphold. Just as the phrase "true believer" can apply to faith in the supernatural, it can also be a trust in the general goodness of life and people.

While working on *True Believer*, Wolff wrote the short story "Religion: From the Greek *Re Legios*, To Re-link," published in *I Believe in Water: Twelve Brushes with Religion* (Singer, 2000). In it, she explores the reactions of three young American teens to an unexpected pregnancy. All three turn to their religious traditions: Deborah, whose knowledge of the Bible indicates a comparatively conservative background, feels guilty that she has related to her God rather casually; Zhandra has studied Buddhism earnestly for a year since her parents have moved their family to an ashram; Riva is a Muslim who studies the Qur'an, following traditional rituals and moral practices of her faith.

Deborah wonders about the very name and nature of God; she has met Jason in her church youth group and tried to protest against anything more than kissing. Yet she alone feels responsibility, especially as Jason has ignored her since knowing about her pregnancy. She also feels a growing affection for the baby growing inside her. She knows that the logical answer is abortion, but she cannot bring herself to extinguish this future life. When her parents realize that she is pregnant, they take time to think about it before they accept Deborah's decision that their family will increase by one, and they will try their best to love this baby. Deborah asks, "Will we be okay, God? . . . The next twenty years will be my hardest job of all. Help me" (Singer, 70).

Zhandra has fallen under the spell of Beni who shushes her into lovemaking. When he finds she is pregnant, he consoles her by telling her that the baby may be the next Buddha; nothing upsets his equilibrium. When he hears about the baby, he advises, "think of the river of life" (Singer, 63). Zhandra decides to mimic his calm acceptance during the months of carrying the baby, which will be adopted by another family in the ashram. She remembers the Zen master who defined life as "one mistake after another" as she watches her father and Beni shoot baskets.

Riva feels guilty and unclean. Ahmad tells her to be silent while he enjoys her body. "God forgives those who truly repent. But human beings are not so forgiving" (Singer, 67), so Riva tries to be brave when Ahmad fearfully moves to another school after she tells him about her pregnancy. She knows that her family will be dishonored and she will never marry. Fortunately, "Allah loosened the baby's grip on [her]" (Singer, 72), and she is saved from the traditional shame by a miscarriage. Even so, she senses that her mother suspects something and hides it from her anxiously fragile father. Riva praises Allah for his wisdom.

In this story, Wolff explores the impact of pregnancy on three traditional ways of believing in God. In all three, the girl bears the social stigma of sex, while the boy escapes any long-term commitment. None of the girls lose faith in God or express any anger. Each is a true believer that her God will help her find a way to survive, just as LaVaughn has faith that new possibilities for joy and laughter and growth will happen. While the faith of Deborah, Zhandra, and Riva in a supreme deity gives them strength, LaVaughn seems to believe in the adequacy of the human world, for she marvels in the complexities of life that she learns in biology, and she trusts in the kindness of the people she knows. It is, of course, a faith that is no more logical than that of Deborah, Zhandra, and Riva. How will her faith be tested in the third volume of the *Make Lemonade* series?

In her story about the inner challenges of pregnancy, Wolff seems to be careful not to privilege one way of faith; yet the parents of Deborah and Zhandra react with strength and acceptance, while Riva doesn't even tell her mother and her mother in turn hides her suspicions from Riva's father. What would have been Riva's fate had the baby not miscarried?

Wolff merely presents the thoughts of each girl without making judgments. In an interview Wolff explained that the ideas for her stories have their source in her own point of view. But as she is writing she tries "to walk around it, trying to see it as a kid or kids would" ("Virginia Euwer Wolff," 1). In this story, as in her other works, Wolff lets her readers draw their own conclusions, yet she gently points the way toward a generous acceptance of life's accidents. Religions that require strict adherence to rules favor a hierarchy of power; they separate people into the obedient and the bad, or into those who can hide their mistakes and those who can't. In *True Believer* LaVaughn rejects that type of faith by refusing to join Myrtle and Annie's organization, ironically named the Joyful Universal Church of Jesus. Wolff describes how the church group finally breaks up after secret meetings at night in a violent demonstration in which the leader is jailed. Like Riva's religion, this church has tried to measure out strict rules of behavior without allowing for the forgiveness of human imperfection and the happenstances of most lives. Wolff indicates that this kind of religion is not an adequate weapon against the chaotic conditions of poverty. It is too rigid, unlike the bamboo mentioned in *The Mozart Season* that symbolizes strength with flexibility. Better is the kind of life that lets in laughter and a sense of joy and beauty to balance the pain.

In her speech to a group of writers, teachers, librarians, and other professionals interested in young adult literature at a meeting of ALAN, Wolff spoke about the despair of children who live amid ugliness with no consciousness of beauty and joy, and of the fear of violence that has become so prevalent in our culture. She read a passage from *True Believer* in which LaVaughn looks down at a beetle struggling over the cracks in the sidewalk, stubbornly persisting in climbing over obstacles, keeping to its path. In the beetle's hard work to keep going, LaVaughn sees a metaphor for the tragedy of life, where the overcoming of obstacle after obstacle nevertheless leads to death. What's the point? She sees life as full of pain and fear, danger and unavoidable disappointment. This kind of despair is real. LaVaughn's question has never been satisfactorily answered—forever and ever, amen. It is the seminal question of most religious traditions. All LaVaughn can believe is that there may be a point; anything is possible.

In that same speech Wolff also read a passage from *Make Lemonade* in which Jolly and LaVaughn join in a bout of joyous laughter, the kind that makes LaVaughn feel that she will be safe forever. Laughter happens when people make contact and share their stories. Deborah and Zhandra tell their parents about their pregnancies, and their parents help them; what at first seemed a pointless tragedy becomes an opportunity for joy because the girls and their families work together. Riva must face her pregnancy alone. The only person she tells is afraid and disappears. Only by accident is her life saved from the tragedy of loneliness and shame.

If Wolff's work is not full of belly laughs, her language certainly dishes up plenty of opportunity for wry smiles. When LaVaughn is falling in love with Jody, when she senses his presence by the chlorine swimming pool smell in the elevator, she admits, "my whole body goes twang" (35). Any reader who has had a knock-your-knees-weak crush on someone else can appreciate that loose-guitar-string feeling. When LaVaughn's mother finds out that the man who has been courting her wants to borrow money from her daughter's college fund, she yells him out the door and dissipates her rage by ironing. "She ironed everything we have that's made of cloth. / She ironed my jeans. My underwear. Dishtowels. / She washed and ironed curtains, / nightgowns, sweatshirts, her bathrobe, my bathrobe. She ironed pot holders and washcloths. / She didn't stop" (187). It's not just the mental image of all this angry ironing that is amusing; it's the rhythm of this song of determination. It sounds as defiant as the lyrics and tune of "I'm Gonna Wash that Man Right Outta my Hair" from Rodgers and Hammerstein's musical opera *South Pacific*. *True Believer* ends on a markedly upbeat note. The club that has filled the minds of Myrtle and Annie with such hatred where there should be love breaks up in a raucous scene LaVaughn and her mother watch on television. And LaVaughn forgives Jody for being himself in the most comic of circumstances.

It is Dr. Rose who puts into words what LaVaughn's mother teaches every day of her life by example and by direction. "We will rise to the occasion, which is life" (153). This becomes the mantra of the class. LaVaughn is not sure she fully comprehends its connotations until she decides to accept Jody as he is, and, rising from underneath the table where she has been cleaning up spilled birthday cake, she introduces him as her friend. Now she knows what it is to "rise to the occasion, which is life." At sixteen, she has come out of a self-imposed exile and can look both backward with fondness and forward with anticipation.

As serious and profound as the themes of Wolff's work are, her language allows for lightness and laughter too. She crafts a whole experience with a story and characters who are more than the simple stick figures of the book's opening image. In the end, Wolff prefers togetherness and laughter to the solitary adherence to someone else's rules. LaVaughn's sixteenth birthday is a gorgeously messy celebration of goodwill, artistic beauty, and friendships crafted by sharing stories.

True Believer has won a large number of awards. In 2001, the book received starred reviews from *Publishers Weekly*, the *School Library Journal*, *The ALA Booklist*, *The Bulletin for the Center of Children's Books*, and *The Horn Book* magazine. That same year, it was also selected for the Leslie Bradshaw Award for Young Readers in Oregon, the School Library Journal Best Book of the Year, and a Bulletin of the Center for Children's Books Blue Ribbon Book. In 2002, it was named as one of YALSA's Top Ten Best Books for Young Adults, an American Library Association Notable Children's Book, and a New York Public Library Book for the Teenager. The book's excellence was recognized with the Golden Kite Award, the Pacific Northwest Bookseller's Award, and as a Printz Award Honor Book. *True Believer* was nominated for many other notable awards and selected as a finalist for several, including the Carnegie Medal. Such a reception for a book with such an unusual format and with such a controversial subject indicates the quality of the writing that can supersede those disadvantages. Critical commentary has focused on the clarity of the images, the satisfactory rhythms and sounds of the language, and the poignancy of the characters' relationships.

Of course, the most notable was the National Book Award for Young People's Literature in 2001. The chair of the Young People's Literature Panel, author Beth Kephart, explained how they selected Wolff's book from over 150 entries. They were seeking "enduring books . . . that enter the bloodstreams of their readers, that stir and shape and finally transform . . . that jolt us toward insight, compassion, . . . toward the answers to the questions we must keep asking" ("Transcript," 2). They selected *True Believer* as "the most fierce, most unyielding, most original,

At the National Book Awards ceremony, Virginia Euwer Wolff stands between her daughter, Juliet Wolff, and her son, Anthony Wolff, on November 14, 2001.

most unafraid to get inside the heart of readers. We chose a tough and equally beautiful book" ("Transcript," 3). The National Book Awards were presented in New York City in November 2001. In her words of acceptance, words that emcee Steve Martin said went from "shocked to eloquent," Wolff referred back to the tragic destruction of the twin tow-ers of the World Trade Center on September 11, 2001. After that event, she had stopped writing for a while; she wondered whether celebration of a book was appropriate in the face of such sorrow. However, earlier that afternoon she and her son Anthony had visited the site of the Trade Center towers, and there she had witnessed the qualities William Faulkner described in his Nobel acceptance speech in 1953. Wolff had posted these on her wall until they were so internalized she no longer needs to see them. "Faulkner's six," as she calls them, are qualities all conscientious authors should exemplify in their writing: love, honor, pity, pride, compassion, and sacrifice.

These are the qualities that give substance and worth to stories well told and lives lived deeply. They keep comedies from being silly and superficial, and tragedies from being ridiculous. Wolff poses many questions in her books, and points to some possible answers. Is there beauty in life? Yes. It is bought with hard work, empathy, and education. Is there an answer for lives sacrificed? Yes. Pity leads to compassion, and sometimes to the joy of a loving relationship that balances the comforts of touching and sharing with the space to grow in different directions. Virginia Euwer Wolff tells her stories in language that leads readers to understand these qualities in some depth. Like Allegra's relationship with Mozart, Wolff has honored Faulkner's technique of creating unique and memorable characters from the inside out, but she has used her own themes and motifs to make that technique her own. Wolff's stories express her own victories over the shock of loss and the pain of loneliness.

At the end of *True Believer*, LaVaughn, reveling in the joyful noise and loving warmth of her birthday party, thinks to herself, "Guy, your daughter is sixteen / How do you feel about that?" (264). For the part of Virginia Euwer Wolff that is related to LaVaughn, I imagine that the answer must be "Pretty good!"

References

Bowlan, Cheryl. "Interview with Eugene Euwer Wolff." Contemporary Authors Online. The Gale Group, 2001. http://www.galenet.com (3 Jan. 2002).

Colburn, Nell. "The Incomparable Wolff." *School Library Journal* 48, no. 2 (February 2002): 54–56.

"PW Talks With Virginia Euwer Wolff." *Publishers Weekly* 247, no. 51 (18 Dec. 2000): 79.

Singer, Marilyn, ed. *I Believe in Water: Twelve Brushes with Religion*. New York: HarperCollins, 2000.

Sutton, Roger. "An Interview with Virginia Euwer Wolff." *The Horn Book* 77, no. 3 (May/June 2001): 280–288.

"Transcript from the 2001 National Book Awards" (14 Nov. 2001), http://209.67.253.214/nbf/docs/nba01_speech_wolff.htm.

"Virginia Euwer Wolff." AuthorChats. (5 Dec. 2001). http://www. authorchats.com/archives/viewArchive.jsp?id=20011205VirginiaEuwer-Wolff.jsp (7 Oct. 2002).

Wolff, Virginia. "Religion: From the Greek *Re Legios*, to Re-Link." *I Believe in Water: Twelve Brushes with Religion*, edited by Marilyn Singer. New York: HarperCollins, 2000.

Wolff, Virginia. "What We Lose, What We Find." Speech presented at The ALAN Breakfast Meeting, National Council of Teachers Conference, Atlanta, Ga., 23 Nov. 2002.

Bibliography

Books by Virginia Euwer Wolff

Bat 6. New York: Scholastic, 1998.
Make Lemonade. New York: Scholastic, 1993.
The Mozart Season. New York: Scholastic, 1991.
Probably Still Nick Swansen. New York: Henry Holt, 1988.
Rated PG. New York: St. Martin's, 1980.
True Believer. New York: Atheneum Books for Young Readers, 2001.

Short Stories by Virginia Euwer Wolff

"Brownian Motion." *Ultimate Sports: Short Stories by Outstanding Writers for Young Adults*, edited by Donald Gallo. New York: Delacorte Press, 1995.

"Chair." *The Color of Absence: 12 Stories about Loss and Hope*, edited by James Howe. New York: Atheneum Books for Younger Readers, 2001.

"Dozens of Roses: A Story for Voices." *One Experience to Another: Award Winning Authors Share Real-life Experiences through Fiction*, edited by M. Jerry Weiss and Helen S. Weiss. New York: Tor, 1997; Forge, 1997, 1999.

"Religion: From the Greek *Re Legios*, to Re-Link." *I Believe in Water: Twelve Brushes with Religion*, edited by Marilyn Singer. New York: HarperCollins, 2000.

"The Un-numbing of Cory Wilhouse." *No Easy Answers: Short Stories about Teenagers Making Tough Choices*, edited by Donald R. Gallo. New York: Delacorte Press, 1997.

"Water." *Girls Got Game: Sports Stories and Poems*, edited by Sue Macy. New York: Henry Holt, 2001.

"A Wing and a Prayer." *Kid's Stuff: Left Bank Collection* Number 6, edited by Linny Stovall. Hillsboro, Ore.: Blue Heron, 1994.

Selected Nonfiction by Virginia Euwer Wolff

"Foreword" in *We're Alive and Life Goes On: A Theresienstad Diary* by Eva Roubickova. New York: Henry Holt, 1998.

"If I Was Doing It Proper, What Was You Laughing At? Some Notes on the Language of Community." *The Horn Book* 74, no. 3 (1 May 1998): 297–308.

"Introduction" to *I'm Nobody! Who Are You?: Poems by Emily Dickinson*, edited by Eric Mesmer. New York: Scholastic, 2002.

"'Noah's Castle' by John Rowe Townsend: A World Too Nasty to Miss Out On." *Lost Masterworks of Young Adult Literature*, edited by Connie S. Zitlow. Lanham, Md.: Scarecrow Press, 2002.

"Rarely Easy and Never Beautiful." *The ALAN Review* (Spring 1991): 2-3.

"What We Lose, What We Find." Speech presented at The ALAN Breakfast Meeting, National Council of Teachers Conference, Atlanta, Ga., 23 Nov. 2002.

About Virginia Euwer Wolff

"An Interview with Virginia Euwer Wolff." http://www.lafsd.k12.ca.us/Stanley/music/Features/Wolff_Interview/index.php. (3 Jan. 2002).

"Virginia Euwer Wolff." AuthorChats. (5 Dec. 2001). http://www.authorchats.com/archives/viewArchive.jsp?id=20011205VirginiaEuwerWolff.jsp (7 Oct. 2002).

Belben, Cathy. "Virginia Euwer Wolff Author Profile." http:/www.be.wednet.edu/Hs/library/virgina_euwer_wolff_author_prof.htm.

Bowlan, Cheryl. "Interview with Eugene Euwer Wolff." Contemporary Authors Online. The Gale Group, 2001. http://www.galenet.com (3 Jan. 2002).

Cart, Michael. "Novels in Verse: A New Trend," *Voices from the Middle* 9, no. 2. (December 2001): 97–98.

Colburn, Nell. "The Incomparable Wolff." *School Library Journal* 48, no. 2 (February 2002): 54–56.

Gallo, Don. "Virginia Euwer Wolff." Interview.Authors4Teens.com. http://www. authors4teens.com/A4T?source=interview&authorid=wolff (16 Jan. 2001).

Hock, Beverly Vaughn. "The Labryinth of Story: Narrative as Creative Construction. A Participatory Study." Dissertation, University of San Francisco, Calif., 1999.

Hughes-Hassell, Sandra, and Sandy L. Guild. "The Urban Experience in Recent Young Adult Novels." The ALAN Review 29, no. 3 (Spring/Summer 2002): 35–39.

McNulty, Mary H. "Music and Truth: Discovery in Three Young Adult Novels." The ALAN Review 27, no. 3 (Fall 1999): 47–50.

Nobles, Susanne. "Why Don't We Ever Read Anything Happy?" The ALAN Review 26 no. 3 (Fall 1998): 46–50.

Olenchak, F. Richard. "When Gifted Readers Hunt for Books." Voices from the Middle 9 no. 2 (December 2001): 71–73.

Pavonetti, Linda M. "Historical Fiction—New and Old." Voices from the Middle 9, no. 2 (December 2001): 78–82.

"PW Talks With Virgnia Euwer Wolff." Publishers Weekly 247, no. 51 (18 Dec. 2000): 79.

Singer, Marilyn, ed. I Believe in Water: Twelve Brushes with Religion. New York: HarperCollins, 2000.

Singer, Marilyn. "What is a Short Story?" The ALAN Review 28, no. 1 (Fall 2000): 38–40.

Sutton, Roger. "An Interview with Virginia Euwer Wolff." The Horn Book 77, no. 3 (May/June 2001): 280–288.

"Transcript from the 2001 National Book Awards" (14 Nov. 2001) http://209.67.253.214/nbf/docs/nba01_speech_wolff.htm.

Zitlow, Connie S. "Sounds and Pictures in Words: Images in Literature for Young Adults." The ALAN Review 27, no. 1 (Winter 2000): 20–26.

Zvirin, Stephanie. "The Booklist Interview: Virginia Euwer Wolff." Booklist. (1 Mar. 1994). 1250–1251.

Other Works Cited

Armor, John, and Peter Wright. Manzanar. Photographs by Ansel Adams. Commentary by John Hersey. New York: Times Books, 1988.

Davis, Daniel. Behind Barbed Wire: The Imprisonment of Japanese Americans During World War II. New York: Dutton, 1982.

Mochizuki, Ken. Baseball Saved Us. Illustrated by Dom Lee. New York: Scholastic, 1993.

Salinger, J. D. "For Esmé—With Love and Squalor." *Nine Stories*. New York: Bantam Books, 1948, 1981. 87–114.

Salinger, J. D. *The Catcher in the Rye*. Boston: Little, Brown, and Company, 1945, 1951.

Index

~

About the Author

Suzanne Elizabeth Reid is an assistant professor at Emory & Henry College in southwestern Virginia where she teaches courses in literature for children and young adults, great books, and teacher preparation. A former teacher of high school English, she has also taught numerous courses in writing and literature at the community college and college level. She has published articles about literacy and education in journals including *The ALAN Review* and *Virginia English Bulletin* and serves on the editorial board of *English Journal*. She is the author of *Presenting Cynthia Voigt, Presenting Ursula LeGuin, Presenting Science Fiction,* and a publication for Scarecrow Press, *Book Bridges: Strategies for Teaching ESL with Children's and Young Adult Literature*.